Customer Satisfaction Toolkit for ISO 9001:2000

Also available from ASQ Quality Press:

Measuring and Managing Customer Satisfaction: Going for the Gold
Sheila Kessler

Customer Satisfaction Measurement Simplified: A Step-by-Step Guide for ISO 9001:2000 Certification
Terry G. Vavra

Improving Your Measurement of Customer Satisfaction: A Guide to Creating, Conducting, Analyzing, and Reporting Customer Satisfaction Measurement Programs
Terry G. Vavra

Analysis of Customer Satisfaction Data
Derek R. Allen and Tanniru R. Rao

Measuring Customer Satisfaction: Survey Design, Use, and Statistical Analysis Methods, Second Edition
Bob E. Hayes

Customer Centered Six Sigma: Linking Customer, Process Improvement, and Financial Results
Earl Naumann and Steven H. Hoisington

ISO 9001:2000 Explained, Second Edition
Charles A. Cianfrani, Joseph J. Tsiakals, and John E. (Jack) West

Value Leadership: Winning Competitive Advantage in the Information Age
Michael C. Harris

To request a complimentary catalog of ASQ Quality Press publications, call 800-248-1946, or visit our Web site at http://qualitypress.asq.org .

Customer Satisfaction Toolkit for ISO 9001:2000

Sheila Kessler

ASQ Quality Press
Milwaukee, Wisconsin

Customer Satisfaction Toolkit for ISO 9001:2000
Sheila Kessler

Library of Congress Cataloging-in-Publication Data

Kessler, Sheila.
   Customer satisfaction toolkit for ISO 9001:2000 / Sheila Kessler.
     p. cm.
   Includes bibliographical references and index.
   ISBN 0-87389-559-2 (Soft cover, ring bind : alk. paper)
   1. Consumer satisfaction—Statistical methods. 2. Questionnaires. 3. Customer services—Quality control. 4. Quality assurance—Management. 5. ISO 9000 Series Standards. I. Title.

HF5415.335 .K467 2002
658.8'12—dc21   2002012071

© 2003 by ASQ

All rights reserved. No part of this book may be reproduced in any form or by any means, electronic, mechanical, photocopying, recording, or otherwise, without the prior written permission of the publisher.

10 9 8 7 6 5 4 3 2 1

ISBN 0-87389-559-2

Publisher: William A. Tony
Acquisitions Editor: Annemieke Koudstaal
Project Editor: Craig S. Powell
Production Administrator: Gretchen Trautman
Special Marketing Representative: David Luth

ASQ Mission: The American Society for Quality advances individual and organizational performance excellence worldwide by providing opportunities for learning, quality improvement, and knowledge exchange.

Attention Bookstores, Wholesalers, Schools, and Corporations: ASQ Quality Press books, videotapes, audiotapes, and software are available at quantity discounts with bulk purchases for business, educational, or instructional use. For information, please contact ASQ Quality Press at 800-248-1946, or write to ASQ Quality Press, P.O. Box 3005, Milwaukee, WI 53201-3005.

To place orders or to request a free copy of the ASQ Quality Press Publications Catalog, including ASQ membership information, call 800-248-1946. Visit our Web site at www.asq.org or http://qualitypress.asq.org .

Printed in the United States of America

 Printed on acid-free paper

American Society for Quality
ASQ

Quality Press
600 N. Plankinton Avenue
Milwaukee, Wisconsin 53203
Call toll free 800-248-1946
Fax 414-272-1734
www.asq.org
http://qualitypress.asq.org
http://standardsgroup.asq.org
E-mail: authors@asq.org

Contents

Preface . . . . **vii**

Chapter 1   Introduction **1**
Why Bother? 1
Guidelines to the Toolkit 1
Key Customer-Related Changes in ISO 9001:2000 2
Easy versus Best-in-Class Tools 3
Customer Satisfaction Surveys 4

Chapter 2   System and Science of Measurement **7**
Segmenting Your Customers: Going for the Gold 7
Measuring Your Customers—Systematically and Scientifically 8
Methods of Sampling 14
Sample Size 15
Survey Construction 16
Response Rates 16
Question Construction 18
Scale Construction 23

Chapter 3   Customer Needs Assessment **27**
Overview 27
Tool #1: Specifications 28
Tool #2: ServQual 29
Tool #3: Quality Function Deployment 31
Tool #4: Discovery Interviews 32
Tool #5: Customer Quick Maps 33
Tool #6: Service Level Agreement 34
Tool #7: Derived Importance (from the Overall Satisfaction Question) 36
Best Practice for Customer Needs Assessment 37

Chapter 4   Customer Satisfaction Measures **39**
Customer Satisfaction Surveys 39
Tool #1: Postcard Type Survey—Easy 40
Tool #2: Written Survey 41
Preparing the Customer for the Survey 47
Tool #3: Phone or In-Person Survey 49
Tool #4: E-Mail Survey—Easy 51

v

Chapter 5   Complaint Resolution Systems **53**
   Best-Practice Complaint Systems 53
   Critical Issues and Tips 55

Chapter 6   Analysis and Decision Making: Balanced Scorecards **57**
   Analysis and Decisions 57
   Sample Results Chart for Customer Needs 58
   Sample Satisfaction Trend Chart 58
   Sample Balanced Scorecard for Strategic Quality Plan Retreat 62
   View Balanced Scorecard Data Simultaneously 63

Chapter 7   Action and Review **65**
   Action: Turning Data into Improvement 65

Appendix **67**
   Glossary of Customer Feedback Tools 68
   ISO 9000:2000 Fundamentals and Vocabulary 73
   Bibliography 78
   Training—Seminars and Web Training 79

Index **81**

Preface

This toolkit integrates ISO 9001:2000 requirements and the best-in-class processes that answer those requirements for measuring and managing customer satisfaction. The key to success is to:

Ask the right questions of the right people in the right way at the right time.

Thus, this book is meant to be a quick and practical guide on such issues as:

- How to select the customers to survey
- How to sample and what sample size is appropriate
- How to design questions so they are clear and relevant
- Which is the most cost effective and beneficial way to deploy the survey (phone, mail, Web, fax, e-mail)
- What are the minimum ISO customer satisfaction requirements in contrast to those processes that lead to financial results
- How to analyze the data
- How to turn the data into action

The design of the book is a concise, toolkit approach for companies or units that want to use the "voice of the customer" to enhance their products and services. The book will be of value to anyone moving into the 2000 version of ISO. Medium-sized companies will find that it simplifies the customer satisfaction requirements in ISO. At the same time, the author has had 20 years of implementing customer satisfaction systems in small, medium, and large Fortune 500 companies.

This book also clarifies the differences between:

Delightful and frightful customer satisfaction systems.

Most everyone reading this book has personally experienced a "frightful" measurement system. Rather than a true system, a frightful one involves surveys that don't ask the right questions of the right people in the right way. Frightful systems also include company systems that do nothing with the data they receive. You will see that you can comply with the ISO 9001 requirement with a "frightful" system.

Token efforts lead to frightful surveys. A token effort will be very apparent to your customers and will irritate them. You can actually drive customers away if you don't do this piece of ISO well. Customer satisfaction measurement should be a window through which your customers and employees see the genuineness of your management's caring about the people they serve.

This book will help you optimize both the customer satisfaction system *and the bottom line.*

Introduction

WHY BOTHER?

When you think about all the extra work that goes into the customer satisfaction requirements in the new ISO standards, you should also consider the payoff. ISO 9001:2000 is very close to the Baldrige Award Criteria in its requirements for a customer-driven organization. Figure 1.1 demonstrates the remarkable payoff that being customer focused has had. It is based on a robust research project done with 600 winners and 600 matched control organizations. Operating income, sales and employee growth, profit, and return on assets (ROA) were all significantly higher with those organizations that met the Award Criteria. The question really is—can you afford *not* to do it?

GUIDELINES TO THE TOOLKIT

This toolkit intends to provide basic tools currently being used in both "easy" and "best-in-class" customer satisfaction systems. In addition to management responsibility, there are three basic systems and tools required by ISO 9001:2000:

1. Customer needs assessment system and measurement

2. Customer satisfaction system and measurement

3. Complaint (inquiries, feedback, dissatisfaction) system and measurement

This toolkit provides the system and tools most commonly found in all three of these customer requirements. The three tools listed above are core to the requirements.

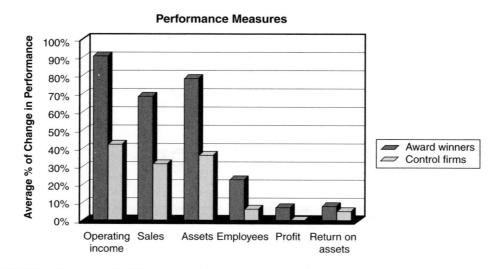

Figure 1.1 Study of 600 Baldrige Award winners and 600 matched controls. Baldrige Award winners scored significantly higher on all measures. Kevin B. Hendricks and Vinod Singhal, "Don't Count TQM Out," *ASQ Quality Progress* (April 1999). Used by permission.

High-performing companies use more than just core tools. The toolkit provides exposure to additional tools as well.

These ingredients and tools include the basic survey design, survey layout, wordcrafting in questions, statistical considerations, typical management review agendas, and how to move from data to action. The toolkit is meant to be used as a resource book.

KEY CUSTOMER-RELATED CHANGES IN ISO 9001:2000

First, it might be helpful to review the key components of the new ISO standard. It is vastly different from the 1994 standard, which concentrated on documenting procedures in job descriptions and the like. The ISO 9001:2000 standard is very integrated compared to the old. The new standard requires that customer needs determine priority processes to monitor. Both quality and customer satisfaction measures determine whether customer needs have been met. And top management has to be a driving force for all of this.

You have to show that *top management not only knows customer needs* but also communicates those needs to the entire organization. Management has to hire and use people that are trained and know what they are doing to drive the customer metrics. The new ISO makes it harder and harder to get by with "The customer is #1" poster-only lip service.

Executive Involvement

Involved executives are imperative for the ISO system to work. They are in charge of communicating the customer needs in the first place. They make sure that the identified needs have processes attached to them that ensure that the requirements are met. They motivate the employees to do this extra work through praise, recognition, awards, promotions, and tangible evidence. They are responsible for knowing how the fixes are coming. ISO requires that the top-level executives be involved. Executives cannot delegate the entire system down.

Difference between ISO 9000, ISO 9001, and ISO 9004

The following table provides the three parts of the new ISO standard:

	Standard	Covers
1.	ISO 9000: 2000	Vocabulary and fundamentals
2.	ISO 9001: 2000	Requirements
3.	ISO 9004: 2000	Performance improvement guidelines (not required)

This toolkit focuses on ISO 9001:2000, since that is where the requirements reside.

Major Changes in ISO 9001:2000

The new (ISO 9001:2000) standard:

1. Focuses on eight quality management principles (customer focus, leadership, involvement of people, process approach, systems approach to management, continual improvement, factual approach to decision making, and mutually beneficial supplier relationships)

2. Requires much more top management involvement

3. Mandates customer focus—with measures and actions required

4. Takes a continuous improvement focus

5. Is simpler: has four key elements instead of 20

6. Is much less prescriptive in documentation: required in six places rather than 18

EASY VERSUS BEST-IN-CLASS TOOLS

Each organization has a choice of how to choose and implement the system requirements. The toolkit presents two different choices for each of the three required areas above:

1. Easy

2. Best-in-class

The easy tools are quite commonly found in organizations worldwide. They do show that the organization has activity in the above area. However, only the best-in-class

4 *Chapter One*

tools have been proven to have a clear and predictable relationship between the tool, true customer satisfaction, and financial results. Thus, using the "easy tool" is at your own risk.

The problems with the "easy" forms of measurement are:

1. They use simple, written generic tools that are not customized to the types of products or requirements specific to the customers. Customers see the superficiality and either don't respond at all or sense that the organization doesn't take customer satisfaction seriously.

2. The questions used are neither actionable nor traceable—so managers don't know what to fix to raise the scores.

3. The "scores" distract top management from the real heart of the system—the fixes. Managers learn how to creatively get good scores by asking easy but irrelevant questions, asking friends of the department, or intimidating customers and employees into giving high scores.

Most often organizations will use the "best-in-class" tools for their key customers and key products and use the easy surveys for those customers and products that are less critical to the organization's success. Best-in-class measures are too expensive to apply to every customer or product. Strategic use of the tools is imperative for success.

Tables 1.1, 1.2, and 1.3 spell out what the measurement tool choices are, the training needed for each tool, and the deployment method most commonly used. These tables are not intended to provide full training in best-in-class tools, but rather basics and exposure to the various choices. See the glossary at the very end of this toolkit for a more comprehensive list of tools, definitions, and details on deployment.

CUSTOMER SATISFACTION SURVEYS

The assumption with customer satisfaction surveys is that they are proactive. Proactive means that the organization reaches out to customers to measure their satisfaction instead of waiting for the customers to comment. Proactive also means that the organization attempts to get a fair representation of its target customers so that the results can be generalized to the rest of the population. *Comment cards sitting in the corner of a room are not customer satisfaction surveys.* Comment cards serve as part of a complaint or customer feedback system—which assumes a passive role of the organization. Comment cards do not represent the customer population fairly—individuals usually are very happy or unhappy when they fill them out.

See Response Rates (page 16) for tips on how to achieve high response rates.

Table 1.1 Easy vs. best-in-class customer needs assessment.

	Level of Difficulty	Tool(s)	Deployment	Training Needed to Deploy	Synthesis
1.	Easy	ServQual (done by neutral person)	Written: mail, fax, or e-mail survey	2 hours	Gap analysis
2.	Best-in-class	Multiple listening posts (several of below)			Pattern analysis of repeat themes—facilitator required
		• Needs assessment, for instance, discovery interview	• Interviews	• 2 days	
		• Quality function deployment (technical)	• Group	• 3–5 days	
		• Focus groups	• Group	• 2 days	
		• Open comments from satisfaction surveys	• Interviews	• 2 hours	
		• Lost customer surveys (usually phone)	• Interviews	• 2–3 days	
		• Sales and frontline input (at meetings/by phone)	• Input from salespeople/ front line	• 2 hours	

Table 1.2 Easy versus best-in-class customer satisfaction surveys.

	Level of Difficulty	Tool(s) & Typical Response Rates	Deployment & Media	Training Needed	Measurement Synthesis to Deploy
1.	Easy	Post card surveys • Mail response rates 10–30% • E-mail 30–70%	Yearly + (mail/e-mail)	1–2 hours	Percentages** or gap analysis
		Generic written surveys, e.g., ServQual (deployed by neutral person via mail or e-mail) • Mail response rates 10–30% • E-mail 30–70%	Yearly + Written survey (mail/e-mail)		
2.	Best-in-class	Customized satisfaction surveys*** (done by a neutral person) • Phone response rates 80–90% • In-person 90%+	Monthly to yearly Phone or in-person	2–3 days	Theme analysis
		Transaction surveys (done by automated system or front line). • In person 80%+ • E-mail 50% • Voice response unit* 80%	At time of transaction—phone, fax, e-mail. Voice response unit	4 hours	Time to complete complaints fixed satisfactorily

* Voice response units (VRUs) are automated phone queries that take and calculate response time and satisfaction levels.

** Percentages mean that questions are analyzed in terms of the percent of respondents that mark "satisfied" or "very satisfied."

*** Customized surveys include questions relevant to specific categories of customer. For instance, in technical products several layers of decision makers usually influence the selection of the supplier. Engineering, the chief financial officer, and the operations manager may all be part of the decision. Each has a different perspective. The questions asked are customized to fit those requirements specific to that person or function.

6 *Chapter One*

Table 1.3 Easy versus best-in-class complaint resolution systems.

	Level of Difficulty	Tool(s)	Deployment	Training Needed to Deploy	Measurement Synthesis
1.	Easy	Comment cards	Written cards	Just question design and analysis—one day	Summary of number and types of comments
2.	Best-in-class	Integrated customer service or call centers • Whole organization involved with fixes • Multiple access points: toll free, Web, fax, e-mail • Trained people answer phone or Web inquiry, either route or answer questions, and fix problems • Automation used but not abused to route calls, track input resolution times, script answers, and provide diagrams • Process owners are accountable for fixes • Standards for problem resolution set for both timing and customer satisfaction • Managers look at patterns of calls and inquiries, and then fix larger issues	Whole organization is trained and involved in fixes and rewarded for their involvement	One to two years—need an expert to guide this process Training for new customer service representative is six weeks to six months	Quick fixes—immediate attention by empowered employees System fixes—pattern analysis done by top management and key initiatives derived from

System and Science of Measurement

SEGMENTING YOUR CUSTOMERS: GOING FOR THE GOLD

Many companies consolidate all their customers into one pool and then randomly select a sample. Yet, the Pareto principle usually applies to a customer base, e.g., "20 percent of the customers account for 80 percent of the revenues." The Gold or heavy users of a service or product can be a vastly different demographic and have different sets of needs than very light users. To combine the two may distort your results so that strategic decisions can be dangerous to the bottom line. You will want to segment your customers so that you can randomly sample within each cluster.

An organization doesn't have to measure either the needs or the satisfaction level of all of its customers. Likewise, an organization may choose to measure one segment more rigorously (higher response rate, use interviews instead of e-mail survey) than another.

You want to measure your customers strategically. Thus, more effort will go into those key products and services you want to grow. More expense may go into measuring those customers who are high revenue, high profit, or high growth for the organization.

Most organizations, after they go through this exercise, discover that their customer segments have different demographics and needs. For instance, casinos know that their heaviest users visit them several times a week, tend to have "addiction" problems, and are older (55 to 70) than their "medium frequency users." The medium frequency users are 35- to 55-year-old professionals, shop for places to entertain themselves and then decide on the casino, and spend less than half the amount that their heavy users do. The least frequent users are people who visit once or twice a year, and are more likely to bring their children. These three groups have very different needs. Thus, the casino has targeted the medium-frequency user group to focus its resources. Most of the clients I have worked with have found clusters of very different client needs based on this stratification.

Other organizations focus on their highest-revenue customers. The billing department usually provides the list of these top-tier customers (usually 20 to 30 percent) who make up 70 to 80 percent of the revenues of the company. Even the largest Fortune 500 companies usually only have a few hundred customers (some only a few dozen) in this category. That high-revenue customer list may be peppered with a few high-growth (but not high-revenue yet) customers. Winnowing down the numbers makes robust measurement very cost-effective.

Thus, however you define your Gold customers, "Go for the Gold!" Define yourself and your target audience. Then measure. As you read through sampling methods, notice that you would use stratified random sampling for your sampling methodology.

MEASURING YOUR CUSTOMERS—SYSTEMATICALLY AND SCIENTIFICALLY

Whether you are measuring customer needs, satisfaction levels, or seeing how well your complaint system works, the same principles apply about being systematic and scientific. The following reviews a few of the principles underlying systematic and scientific measures of customers.

Systematic

First, every system has a purpose. What is the purpose of measuring your customer's needs and satisfaction? If your sole purpose is any of the following you will have a problem financially benefiting from your system:

1. Keeping score

2. Marketing (to say you are measuring)

3. Serving your own management

4. Being totally responsive to your customers

5. Complying with ISO 9001:2000

The scorecard will only give you clues; it is not the purpose of measurement. Many companies set targets for customer satisfaction scores and lose sight of the customers in the process. Managers are not rewarded for fixing problems, but for scores. If a scorecard is your purpose, you will develop an organization that is excellent at manipulating the questions, the deployment, and the results so the scores come out well. How many times have you seen a company advertise that their customer satisfaction scores are high—while you are having a terrible experience with them and so is everyone around you?

In my book, *Measuring and Managing Customer Satisfaction: Going for the Gold,* this result is called the "fools' gold" system. Only a few of the naïve insiders are deluded that it has any value. The same happens with the purpose of marketing and serving your own management. High scores open doors. You won't have to look at your scorecard—just listen to your customers, suppliers, and own employees talk about their delight. You see it in the financial performance. If your purpose is truly customer focus, then the organization radiates this heartfelt desire.

Likewise, some organizations confuse being totally responsive to their customers with being customer focused. While responsiveness is a great trait to have, being overly responsive tends to abuse your larger customer and employee base. One data service company, for instance, processed transactions for a bank. The bank would feed its records to them full of errors. The records would be returned, processed, but full of the same errors originally submitted. The bank would constantly be calling for instant rework as irritated customers discovered the faulty work. The data service company would dutifully oblige.

The bank finally fired the data service company. They hired a new one. This time the new data service company set standards for proofing the records before it received them. The service company had procedures it enforced with the bank. The bank needed to be coached on how to use systems with standards. The bank was much happier with the tremendous reduction of infuriated customers created by this new "error-free" relationship. In the words of the bank CEO, "Responsiveness did not serve us. We needed a service company that could force us to step up to being more professional." Other examples abound where organizations spend way too much time on a few abusive customers and neglect their key customers. Setting expectations for response time and delivering on that serves the entire group of customers. Having a system that allows for "special occasion" responsiveness is in the same league.

Systematic also means having the discipline to measure at predefined intervals. The intervals of measurement are based on how frequently your customer bases' needs change. Some companies, like Solectron, measure satisfaction every month, others once a year. Ask your key customers how often they want to be surveyed. Project companies, for instance, engineering firms, usually have customized measurement plans unique to each major project.

10 *Chapter Two*

If you have a systems approach, your customers will find *consistency*—no matter what they touch in the organization. The excellence won't vary—despite the:

- Individual serving them

- Department they are dealing with

- Project that is current

- Location they are using

- New managers

- Season or shift

- Different products or services

Why? Because you *use the same system throughout the organization*. Figure 2.1 shows the various steps in the closed-loop system.

The following table elaborates more fully on the various steps in the system:

Step	What	Explanation
1.	Customer satisfaction plan	First, the executives or those in charge of customer satisfaction need to devise a *customer satisfaction plan*. The commitments that go into the plan are usually decided at a one- to two-day *strategic quality planning retreat*.
2.	Measure and manage	Processes that measure customer needs and satisfaction are included in the quality measures.
3.	Analyze and synthesize data	Customer data needs to support decision making about where the company spends resources. Do you need a better-trained sales staff? Do you need to expand the hours of customer service? Do you need additional features on your product?
4.	Set standards and track	After decisions are made on standards and processes to foster customer satisfaction, they are tracked to ensure they meet their objective. Standards may vary from how long the pricing department has to review a quote to the time it takes to repair a product.
5.	Celebrate	Celebration means making the people who have done the most visible to others. Results need to be communicated to managers, employees, and customers. Celebrating improvement efforts helps to keep employees motivated.

Figure 2.1 Customer satisfaction system.

Customer Satisfaction Plan

One of the best ways of being systematic is to have a customer satisfaction plan. It allows you to organize your steps for an ISO audit as well as incorporate ISO requirements. A table of contents for a customer satisfaction plan might look like this:

1. Start with your *mission and vision.*
2. State your *target products.*
3. Identify who your *target customers* are for those products.
4. Find out what the target *customers' needs* (and *attributes of those needs*) are.
5. Tie the customer needs to specific processes. Set up *monitoring devices.*
6. Specify *methodology* to be used on the surveys, measures, or monitors.
7. Create a *flowchart* to show interactions.
8. Show a *responsibility matrix*: who will do what to whom.
9. Create a *Gantt chart* to show schedule.
10. Spell out *executive and management review* of data and improvements.
11. Include your *communication and celebration plan.*
12. Identify *resources* you will need (software, office privacy, travel).

Figure 2.2 displays a sample flowchart that shows the steps and interactions between participants.

A sample customer satisfaction responsibility matrix fulfills the requirement that "the interaction between the processes of the quality management system" is defined. Figure 2.3 displays an abbreviated sample matrix for a dental clinic. The measures are based on customer needs found in the needs assessment phase. Note that the persons responsible for customer-related processes are clearly identified. See Figure 2.3.

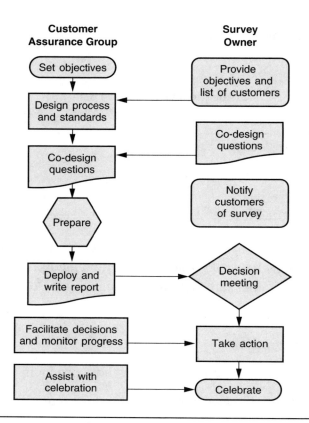

Figure 2.2 Sample customer satisfaction flowchart.

	Measure/Function	Owner	Results Given To	Due By
1.0	Management			
1.1	Executive commitment speech	President	All hands meeting	September meeting
1.2	Customer list and needs	Loyalty manager	All hands meeting	September meeting
1.3	Design of system and changes	Loyalty manager	Steering group	August 15
2.0	Specific Measures			
2.1	Customer satisfaction survey	Sally Green	Partners	Yearly retreat
2.2	Office wait time	Peter Fitch	Dr. Medley/staff	Monthly staff mtg.
2.3	Appointment wait time	Peter Fitch	Dr. Medley/staff	Monthly staff mtg.
2.4	Rework	Li Wang	Partners	Quarterly retreat

Figure 2.3 Customer satisfaction responsibility matrix.

Science

ISO 9001 is designed so that customers' needs are the centerpiece of product and service development and improvement. The science of measuring customers' needs and satisfaction levels takes on a whole new importance when it is being used to determine the organization's future.

> *It is better* not *to measure customer needs and satisfaction than to do a poor job. Cutting corners will irritate your customers (it's very transparent) and undermine strategic decisions on where to put your resources.*

Science is about making the world predictable. A manager's job is to know that if he or she does X, Y is more likely to happen. Good customer satisfaction measurement provides actionable results that lead to increased satisfaction and spending. Statistical techniques make predictions possible.

Statistics

If you are a very small company with 10 key clients, many of the statistical issues will not be relevant. You will be measuring all 10 of your key customers, not sampling them. The more customers you have, the more "statistics" can help you be both cost-effective and timely in your measurement. Good statistics and sampling techniques allow you to generalize to the rest of your customers. First, though:

1. Decide on "confidence level" and "error of the mean"

2. Decide on the sampling method

3. Determine the viable sample size

4. Calibrate the appropriate response rate

Confidence level applies to how confident you want to be with the results. If you set a 95 percent confidence level, it is saying that you are confident that if you repeated the same survey to the same people in the same way, that 95 percent of the time the results would be the same. The higher the confidence level you choose, the more individuals you will need in your sample.

Error of the mean communicates statistically what range or precision you are willing to deal with. If you found that your customer satisfaction scores were 100, you might stipulate five as your error of the mean. With a confidence level of 95 percent, you would be saying that 95 times out of 100 you would find the average score in the sample plus or minus five points from 100. Thus, the range of scores should be 95–105 nearly 95 percent of the time.

One of the most common mistakes organizations make when doing statistical sampling in customer satisfaction measurement is to accept a response rate of 20 percent, 60 percent, or even 80 percent. Statistical theory assumes that if you *sample* your customers, *you need 100 percent response rate from that sample to achieve your confidence level.*

METHODS OF SAMPLING

Organizations may find that they can use statistical sampling methods to decrease the costs of measuring customer needs and satisfaction. Stratified random sampling, described below, helps the organization focus on the vital few that usually provide 80 percent of the revenues.

	Method of Sampling	What It Is	When Used
1.	Random sampling	Assign numbers to individuals and then draw numbers out of a hat. Computers can also generate random numbers.	Random selection is the best method when you want to generalize your results to a larger population.
2.	Stratified random sampling	You divide your customers into logical groups and then randomly select within the group. The most customary: • Revenues (high-, middle-, and low-revenue customers) • Profits (most profitable, middle, and least) • Growth (highest growth, middle, and lowest)	Used to avoid an overrepresentation of your lowest-revenue, least profitable, and typically most demanding customers. This method helps you focus on those customers who will bring you the most success. You can "go for the Gold" in your measurement system. You aim for a higher response rate (typically 80 percent) in the Gold band and may settle for 50 percent or below in the lowest tier. You also may interview these people in person or by phone and use an e-mail survey with the lowest band.
3.	Convenience	Customers are chosen because they are convenient to reach. It can lead to highly biased results.	Used when random sampling is not available, is too expensive, or takes too long. Results need to be validated.
4.	Replacement	You have 1000 customers in your total "Gold" population. You determine you want to sample 300. You call 300 and 150 aren't easily available. You keep drawing new names out of the hat until you reach 300.	Replacement sampling is a well-kept secret of many marketing research firms. It is not random sampling! Random sampling requires that you persist with each one that is randomly chosen. It may take 7–10 calls to get through. That persistence is expensive for market research firms so they use replacement sampling. Be sure to cross-validate the findings if this is your methodology. You could have a very biased sample and, thus, unreliable results.

SAMPLE SIZE

The number of customers sampled depends on how high the stakes are for your results. If you are going to spend millions of dollars to change tooling to meet specific customer needs, precision is required. If you are working on a new device to dispense medicine, for instance, a patch or drip, you may want a very high level of precision. On the other hand, customer needs may involve what kind of shrubbery they like outside their new building. Shrubbery can be changed at moderate expense if the results are not correct.

The confidence level indicates a desired level of certainty about the results. At a 95 percent confidence level, the researcher is 95 percent certain that the data is accurate. Increased confidence levels require increased sample sizes. If the stakes are high (large capital expenditures in a new product or distribution channel, high physical risks in a new medical product), the confidence levels need to be very high. You see confidence levels in many of the Harris polls located at the bottom of the results table.

Confidence level is very dependent on the size of the sample. The following shows the relationship between population size and required number of respondents to achieve a 95 percent confidence level.

Sample size requirements at 95 percent confidence level are:

	Population Size	Minimum #		Population Size	Minimum #
1	100	80	6	2000	323
2	200	132	7	5000	347
3	500	218	8	10,000	370
4	1000	278	9	20,000	377
5	1500	306	10	1,000,000	1000

Even more important is the persistence with which you go after your sample. Accepting a 10 percent return rate on a 30 percent sample is not worth your trouble. The 10 percent who happen to respond could all represent a very biased sample (complainers) and not be fully representative. Use your resources to obtain at least an 80 percent return on whatever sample size you choose. Achieving an 80 percent return rate is done by letting customers know you will be sampling them, offering some incentive for participating, and persisting when they are either not easily reached or don't return the questionnaire.

SURVEY CONSTRUCTION

Survey construction can make a huge difference in whether customers will respond and how they will view the professionalism of your survey process. Having a cluttered, disorganized survey will be immediately apparent to a respondent and will influence their decision to participate.

The typical logic in constructing the survey is as follows. Figure 2.4 shows a checklist to make sure you have the essential ingredients.

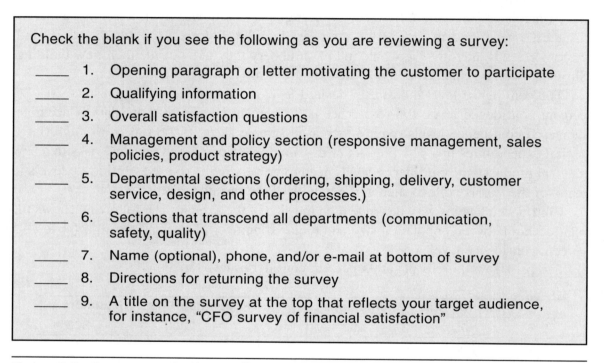

Figure 2.4 Survey organization and logic checklist.

RESPONSE RATES

Response Rates—Tiered

Response rates are the percentage of those that you sampled who actually responded. What percentage of the sample answered your questions, whether by mail, e-mail, phone, or fax? Remember, statistically you need a 100 percent response rate to say that you have sampled a population and can say with XX percent certainty, for instance, 95 percent, that your numbers are within a certain range. This isn't practical in business. Based on best practice, here are the more achievable and yet viable response rates:

1. Gold customers   80%+
2. Second-tier customers   50%+
3. Third-tier customers   30%+

For Gold customers, aim for 100 percent and settle for 80 percent. Even though statistically you may only need 80 percent, Gold customers tend to talk to each other and will be upset if they haven't been included. To achieve this response rate, expect to call multiple times. In high-tech firms you may average six to eight attempts before you finally reach them. It usually doesn't work well to leave a callback if you are long distance—even if you have an 800 number. The time is more costly than the savings with the 800 number. Thus, just keep trying.

At the other end, a 30 percent response rate only gives you a clue what this group is really about. If you want to take the information seriously, you will need to cross-validate the data just to see whether it is worth generalizing. Many companies look at the names in their second-, and third-tier group and see if any are good "potential Gold" customers. If so, they get included as Gold customers and sampled accordingly. Many organizations do not sample or survey their second- and third-tier customers at all.

Tips for Increasing Response Rates:

1. *Loyal and heavy-user customers* are much more willing to participate than low-volume users of your product or service. That is why segmenting your customers and focusing on high-return customers has multiple payoffs—it's easier and more valuable to know what their needs are.

2. The biggest incentive for participating is *making a difference*. Communicate back to your customers how their input made a difference in your product or service design.

3. Catch them in a *captive place*, for instance, waiting in line, before the seminar ends, or "on hold" on the phone. They will be much more likely to participate.

4. Motivate them to participate with a *strong reason*. "We have selected you because you are a valuable customer. We are in the process of revising our products/services and want to tailor them more particularly to our customers' needs. We plan to review this information in June and will be letting you know what the results were." Ask them if they want to see the results. You can even post it to your Web page and tell them when it will be available. Strong causes are more powerful motivators than token sums of money or prizes.

5. If you are asking people to participate in a focus group or lengthy phone call, sometimes a *drawing* works better than offering money. Let them know that they will be entered into a drawing for $100 or more and it will be held on a certain date.

6. If customers have very little of their success dependent on your product, you will have to offer them more to participate in any kind of meaningful research. *Going rates for focus groups* are about $100 to $150 per person. Keep in mind that you will pay this anyway in loss of productivity of the person who has to make 100 phone calls instead of 10 to get participants.

QUESTION CONSTRUCTION

No matter what type of needs assessment or customer satisfaction survey you are doing, question construction is important.

Sequence of Questions

When in a focus group, ask open-ended questions first. Open-ended questions are questions such as: "What do you consider most important?" "What are the main features you would like to see in this product?" Then probe with your specific question, "Would you like a larger size for slightly more money?"

Sensitive Information

1. Put areas like salary categories at the end of the survey.
2. Ask questions regarding salary in multiple choice categories.
3. State the purpose of the question to make it easier to know what you will use the information for.
4. Make sure you are in a private setting.
5. Ask whether you have permission to ask about sensitive topics.

Confidentiality and Expectations

Share your policy on whether or not the information will be confidential. Either way, say that the results will be rolled up and reviewed by management. Also let customers know that all individual preferences will be incorporated, but you are looking for patterns. Then the customers will realize that all of their suggestions will not *automatically* be used.

Content of Questions

The *content of the questions* is determined by the customer needs assessment that you did. You want to track areas that are important to customers. You use the qualitative measures covered in chapter 3, Needs Assessment, to determine what questions to include.

Qualitative measures are open-ended questions on surveys, focus interviews/groups, and employee contacts with customers. Some of the best customer satisfaction system information comes from qualitative measures—because *the customers drive qualitative measures*. Questions come from the customers, not from pre-designed quantitative surveys that box customers into a rating scale. Qualitative measures are quantified through cluster analysis, check sheets, and decibel analysis.

As a result of these qualitative measures, you may have found that these were the key issues identified as important:

Sales service	Pricing	User-friendliness
Ordering accuracy	Warranty	Change process
Availability of product	Quality	Invoices
Technical support	Safety	Process improvement

Say "better technical support" is the main customer complaint in your needs assessment. It is the most frequent need and the most passionate. Give more space in your survey to those loud issues—if they need it. Many times, too few questions are asked about priority areas and too many questions are asked about the unimportant.

Types of Questions

- Qualifying questions

- Branching questions

- Overall customer satisfaction questions

- Open-ended questions

- Pricing questions

Qualifying Questions

You need to know who is filling out the survey. Even if you have the information, you will need to verify some of it. The following demographics or pieces of customer information may prove helpful in analyzing your data later on:

- Position in company

- Location

- When the customer last used the product or service

- How frequently the customer uses the product or service

- Age, income, number of children or any other *relevant* demographics

Branching or Skip Box Questions

Branching or skip box questions are those questions that allow respondents to skip over irrelevant areas. They are a lot easier to use on the phone, in-person, or on e-mail surveys than on written surveys. However, you still see them on written surveys. Example:

> *If you requested repair service, please fill out questions 16 to 20. If not, skip to question 21.*

A Web survey will do the same thing by automatically skipping questions 16 to 20 if the person says they did not request repair service. Not all Web survey software offers "branching." It is an important criterion for selecting the right software.

Overall Customer Satisfaction Questions

Overall customer satisfaction questions are the most important on the survey. They are usually asked with a *Likert scale*. A Likert scale uses a continuum of "very dissatisfied" to "very satisfied" or "strongly disagree" to "strongly agree."

If you really want to test loyalty, three overall satisfaction questions are asked and the answers are averaged for an overall loyalty score. The three questions are as follows:

1. *My overall satisfaction with product or service X was:*
   ❑ *Very dissatisfied* ❑ *Dissatisfied* ❑ *So-so* ❑ *Satisfied* ❑ *Very satisfied*

2. *I would use the service or product again.*
   ❑ *Strongly disagree* ❑ *Disagree* ❑ *So-so* ❑ *Agree* ❑ *Strongly agree*

3. *I would recommend this service or product to others.*
   ❑ *Strongly disagree* ❑ *Disagree* ❑ *So-so* ❑ *Agree* ❑ *Strongly agree*

The combined average of questions one, two, and three is sometimes called the *customer satisfaction index.* You don't need to ask all three overall satisfaction questions if you want to keep the survey short.

The *placement of the main overall satisfaction question* is important. If it is placed at the beginning, the person being surveyed usually gives the most comprehensive and honest response. If it falls at the end, customers are more likely to be influenced by both the questions and their own marks.

Notice that the *sequence of choices* go from low (very dissatisfied) on the left to high (very satisfied) on the right. Placing them in the opposite fashion usually increases the score because people read from left to right.

A *value question* might also provide clues about the customers' view of the features/price tradeoff. Example:

Please rate the value you received relative to the price paid.
❑ *Very dissatisfied* ❑ *Dissatisfied* ❑ *So-so* ❑ *Satisfied* ❑ *Very satisfied*

The overall satisfaction question is used for *trend charts* over quarters or years. A trend chart is illustrated in Figure 2.5. The reason why is that overall satisfaction captures the entire buying experience—both the emotional and the substantive aspects. The overall satisfaction score is much more highly related to repeat buying behavior than any other single question. Likewise, focusing on that one question allows companies to vary the questions they are asking—depending on the position of the customer or the function.

For instance, say your company sells telecom equipment to Baby Bells. Decision criteria are usually mixtures of engineering, project management, software, hardware, finance, and quality. Thus, you may be surveying three different customers in the same company about their satisfaction. One would focus on engineering questions, and another on finance. Just using the overall satisfaction question allows you to integrate the customized surveys.

Usually after the overall question(s) are clusters of questions that relate to both departments and elements of the company that transcend the departments. Clustering is helpful for several reasons. People organize their thoughts (sometimes) around themes. Respondents don't skip around with clusters. Scales remain consistent. Another benefit is that it is easier to feed the information back into the company. Sections can be given to appropriate departments.

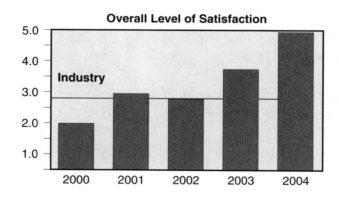

Figure 2.5 Customer satisfaction trend chart.

Open-Ended Questions or Request for Comments

Every written survey needs at least one open-ended question and space for respondents to:

- Clarify their ratings

- Express concerns that were not covered by the questions

- Acknowledge successes

The only exception to this is if you follow up e-mail or written surveys with phone calls. Watch for too much or too little space for comments. Too much space might scare respondents away because it looks too time consuming. Too little space doesn't give the respondent room to say what they want to say. *Three or four lines are plenty.*

Typical open-ended questions or requests for information are:

Please describe what you liked best.

Please share what needed improvement.

Other comments or suggestions?

Sometimes companies only include room for a negative question, for instance, "What needed improvement?" Including room for positive comments is just as important as including room for negative ones. It is easier to increase the positive than change the negative. In addition, morale goes down if surveys are aimed at just finding problems.

Following are some of the common errors made in question design:

	Error	Example	Comment
1	Ambiguous	Was the service professional?	What does professional mean?
2	Not actionable	Was our delivery on time?	What was the expectation?
3	Double questions	Was our service fast and courteous?	Which question is being answered?
4	Scale doesn't match	How satisfied with the product were you?	___ Yes ___ No
5	Biased	Do you feel your rights should be violated?	Who is going to say no?
6	Pricing	Would you like the price to be less?	Why not?
7	Choices not equal	Which of the following is most important to you: 1) reliability, 2) color, 3) shape	Need tougher choices
8	No overall question	How satisfied are you with X?	Most important question
9	No qualifying questions	Frequency of use, demographic information	Important for need stratification

24 *Chapter Two*

SCALE CONSTRUCTION

Following are the various scales and how they are best used.

Likert Scale

Questions using the Likert scale (the most popular scale) are best used for general questions. They can be used on any media, for instance, phone, e-mail, mail, or in-person. N/A means not applicable or no opinion.

1. *The food was served warm*
    ❏ *Strongly agree*   ❏ *Agree*   ❏ *So-so*   ❏ *Disagree*   ❏ *Strongly disagree*   ❏ *N/A*

2. *The answers were accurate*
    ❏ *Strongly agree*   ❏ *Agree*   ❏ *So-so*   ❏ *Disagree*   ❏ *Strongly disagree*   ❏ *N/A*

The five-point Likert scale offers accurate calibration of the answers. According to Likert, having more than five points does not necessarily increase accuracy.

Multiple Choice

A multiple choice scale is best for specific questions on operational definitions and standards you are setting for various customer preferences.

What is your preference in delivery time?
a. *8–10 a.m.*
b. *10–12 a.m.*
c. *1–3 p.m.*
d. *3–5 p.m.*

The multiple choice scale is also used for qualifying questions to determine age, sex, or other demographic brackets.

Yes/No

Following is an example of how a yes/no question could be better worded for more precise calibration.

OK: Have you used product/service X in the past six months: ❑ *Yes* ❑ *No*

Better: How many times have you used product/service X in the past six months? (please check) ❑ *Once* ❑ *Twice* ❑ *Three or more*

Paired Choice

If you had to choose between the following two features of the cell phone if the price were the same, which would you choose? (check one)
a. ❑ *E-mail*
b. ❑ *Internet connection*

The paired-choice scale is good for pricing questions because pricing is usually a price vs. features tradeoff.

Rank Order and Weighted Importance

Weighted importance provides much better calibration for needs assessment than does rank order.

Rank Order Scale

Please rank order the following five features in priority order:

a. Auto mileage
b. Safety
c. Seat comfort
d. Head room
e. Ability to seat six people

1. _____ (most preferred)
2. _____
3. _____
4. _____
5. _____ (least preferred)

Weighted Distribution Scale

Please distribute 100 points among the following five features according to how important each is to you. The total points should add up to 100.

	Feature	Points
	Feature	*Points*
1.	*Auto mileage*	_____
2.	*Safety*	_____
3.	*Seat comfort*	_____
4.	*Head room*	_____
5.	*Ability to seat six people*	_____

Total points   *100*

Customer Needs Assessment

OVERVIEW

According to Dr. Noriaki Kano, a Japanese expert in quality, satisfaction and customer needs are not on a single continuum. Figure 3.1 illustrates three types of customer quality:

1. Expected quality
2. Desired quality
3. Excited quality

When you check into a hotel room, you expect that there will be a blanket on the bed. If the basic requirement is met, the organization does *not* get any more points in customer satisfaction for making that blanket bigger. Once you have met the requirement, satisfaction doesn't go up by doing extras. Desired quality, on the other hand, is a linear scale. The better you are, the happier the customers are. Less time spent waiting at the check-in line at the hotel is an example. Excited quality is when you delight a customer with something they weren't expecting, for instance, a Mrs. Fields' cookie while waiting in line.

By definition, "expected quality" is what customers "must" have when they buy. After you have discovered those "musts" in lost customer interviews, product returns, and what customers report, measure the "musts" through your quality measures. An example of embedding a "must" in a quality measure is at many fast food restaurants. First, the fast food restaurants surveyed customers to define how many minutes "fast" really meant. The clock then records whether or not the drive-through meets that specification. You don't have to waste the customer's time by asking this question in a survey.

28 Chapter Three

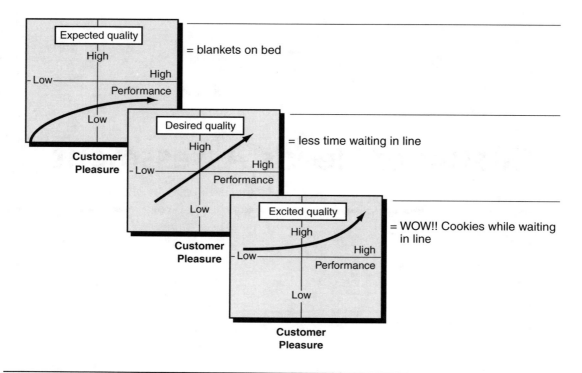

Figure 3.1 Customer satisfaction—not a single concept.

Focus your questions in your customer satisfaction surveys on the *desired* area. Too many surveys ask questions that are "must" questions, for instance, "Is our fast food restaurant fast?" "Did our VCR work when you plugged it in?" "Were our invoices correct?"

Your survey will gain greater customer respect if it focuses on differentiators between you and the competition.

TOOL #1: SPECIFICATIONS

Tool #1 for customer needs assessment is *customer specifications*. Customer specifications, or "specs," is the traditional tool used by organizations to specify their requirements to their suppliers. Typically these specs are part of the request for proposal or request for quote. Customers and suppliers will negotiate the addition, subtraction, or alteration of these specs according to trade-offs with other customer needs and price.

Regulations, laws, and other obligations are also found in customer specifications. Standards (for instance, ANSI standards) are yet another requirement that may be spelled out in contractual specifications. See Figure 3.2 for some sample specifications.

This area is familiar to all companies who do business-to-business contracts. Manufacturers are further ahead than service companies on clearly defining their needs. Note the differences in how long it takes to install a new business phone based on where a company is located. If customer expectations have been measured, they aren't being consistently used as benchmarks. Service companies such as airlines are just starting to get publicity about what customers expect as basic requirements in such things as overbooking, on-time arrivals and departures, lost luggage, and hotel reservations that are given away. Thus, service has a long way to go to narrow the gap between what is expected and what is delivered. Unfortunately, this issue has made customer satisfaction drop considerably in recent years as telecommunication companies have focused on dominance, mergers, market share, and Wall Street. Government is sitting on the sidelines with possible regulations in mind if self-regulation doesn't accelerate.

Thus, customer specs are very common in technical and increasingly common in service contracts. Customized products or services are particularly dependent on well-defined specifications to ensure customer satisfaction. The next tool for needs assessment, a ServQual survey, tries to unearth what is important to the customer through a written survey.

	Type	Name	Abbreviation	How Stated	How Used
1	Technical	Mean time between failure	MTBF	10,000 hours	Reliability measure
2	Service	Wait time	Wait	10–20 min	Customer wait time
3	Law	Speed limit	MPH	65 MPH	On highways
4	Regulation	Particles per million	ppm	30,000 ppm	Toxic emissions

Figure 3.2 Sample specifications.

TOOL #2: SERVQUAL

Figure 3.3 presents a quick and easy way of measuring the importance and satisfaction of needs. The ServQual method shown in Figure 3.3 allows organizations to do a gap analysis and analyze the critical areas needed for improvement (and the bragging points!). This may be a beginning point for companies but does not represent a robust way of finding out customer needs. We have found in 20 years of research that this approach provides very little insight into relevant customer needs. If compiled in-house, the needs listed in the left column typically represent a 20 to 40 percent overlap with the customers' stated needs. In addition, customers tend to rate everything as a four or five in importance. Keep in mind, "Customers want it all, want it now, and provided in the way they want it." In other words, *everything* is important. Thus, the simplicity of the scale can lead customer researchers to assume they now know customer needs when they don't.

Quality function deployment and best-in-class needs assessment create more calibrated customer understanding and lead to better financial results. How? Truly understanding customer needs and applying them to improved products means companies can charge more—especially if that company is the only one attending to those specific needs. More profit usually means more shareholder investment. The results we have personally witnessed during the past 20 years have varied from 30 percent increase in profitability after a year to a fivefold increase in market cap (shareholder investment). The Baldrige results graph at the beginning of this book (Figure 1.1, page 2) adds further credibility to this relationship.

At one end of the difficulty spectrum is ServQual—at the other end is Tool #3, quality function deployment.

Please circle the following numbers that best represent the degree of importance that each category has to you (first set of numbers) and your rating on performance (second set of numbers).

	Degree of Importance to Me (1 = unimportant to 5 = very important)					Satisfaction Rating (1=very unsatisfied to 5=very satisfied)				
1. Facilities are clean	1	2	3	4	5	1	2	3	4	5
2. Employees are neatly dressed	1	2	3	4	5	1	2	3	4	5
3. Employees respond in a timely manner	1	2	3	4	5	1	2	3	4	5
4. Invoices are easy to understand	1	2	3	4	5	1	2	3	4	5
5. Answers to questions are accurate	1	2	3	4	5	1	2	3	4	5
6. Employees are courteous	1	2	3	4	5	1	2	3	4	5
7. Problem solving is customer oriented	1	2	3	4	5	1	2	3	4	5
8. Operating hours are convenient	1	2	3	4	5	1	2	3	4	5
9. Manuals are easy to follow	1	2	3	4	5	1	2	3	4	5
10. Customers receive personal attention	1	2	3	4	5	1	2	3	4	5
11. Safety is emphasized	1	2	3	4	5	1	2	3	4	5
12. Employees understand my needs	1	2	3	4	5	1	2	3	4	5
13. The service is prompt	1	2	3	4	5	1	2	3	4	5

Figure 3.3 ServQual needs assessment (and satisfaction) sample.
The trademark ServQual is held by Zeitmal.

TOOL #3: QUALITY FUNCTION DEPLOYMENT

Figure 3.4 is an illustration of quality function deployment (QFD), a tool that is used in some best-practice companies to do needs assessment. It is particularly helpful in defining how technical specifications relate to lay language. For instance, a customer might say that they wanted a comfortable bed and bedding in a hotel room. When asked to define comfortable bedding, they might say, "You know, sheets that aren't prickly." When further testing that need, you find that sheets that have fewer than 300 threads per inch feel prickly to customers. The 300 threads per inch becomes a specification in purchasing sheets for your hotel. A second need might be a "responsive front desk." Responsive would be defined further as answering the phone in fewer than two rings. The legends in Figure 3.4 explain the other columns and their meaning.

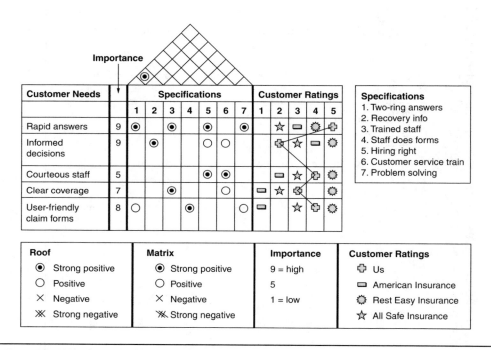

Figure 3.4 Quality function deployment.

TOOL #4: DISCOVERY INTERVIEWS

Introduction

Discovery interviews are in-person or phone discussions with customers for the purpose of discovering their stated or unstated needs.

If the customer is a new customer and you are competing for the job, this interview is best done prior to the proposal or quote.

Customers haven't always thought through what they want, especially in service areas. Yet they will assume that their supplier is able to read their minds. Customers vary greatly in issues such as how much information they need, how they like reports to look, how much input they want to give, and how the final product or service will look. Discovery that happens later in the job usually results in rework and customer dissatisfaction.

Estimates of how much time are taken up by this rework run as high as 40 percent of the total time in services. Thus, defining customer needs up front is a critical area. Specifications are fairly routine. The discovery interview helps you fill in the blanks on all the other requirements.

Steps

1. Set yourself up for success. Ask to meet in a quiet, neutral place away from the distractions of ringing phones and other individuals dropping in. State the purpose of the interview, for instance, "to be more responsive in the proposal" or "to be more responsive in the product or service design." Let them know about how long it will take. Usually 20 minutes is a minimum.

2. At the beginning of the interview, restate the purpose and estimated length. Start out with open-ended questions, like: "First, would you please help me understand what is important to you in the selection of a manufacturer/service provider."

3. As they talk, probe for understanding. What, specifically, does being "responsive" mean? Does that mean returning phone calls within 24 hours? Does it mean being available for meetings with one-day notification?

4. Summarize your understanding of what they said. Sometimes this helps them be even clearer about what they are trying to communicate.

5. After they have finished talking about what they want to talk about, ask other open-ended questions, for instance, "Are there other areas we haven't discussed that are keys to the success of this project/product?"

6. At the end, you might have trigger words that probe areas not covered by the client. They may fall in the areas of:

- Ordering the service or product (how, when, to whom, changes)

- Delivering the service or product (expected turnaround times)

- Expected levels of inventory availability

- Best ways of communicating changes in the product/service/management of your company, for instance, by phone, fax, newsletter

- Problem solving: who will receive queries and complaints, who will pay for their resolution, and what escalation policies are in effect

- Materials you will need from the customer and by when you will need them

- Training available and required

- Use of their personnel to do certain parts of the job

- Inspections—at their site and of their product or service

- Product or service testing

- Closeout or product/service acceptance procedure

- Document contents and control

The path from what customers reveal in the discovery interview to operational standards is via the customer quick maps described in Tool #5.

Customer Needs Assessment **35**

TOOL #5: CUSTOMER QUICK MAP

Figure 3.5, a *customer quick map*, turns stated customer needs into requirements. The requirements are always stated in terms that can be measured. Thus, the organization has the ability to monitor whether the need is being met. You do not have to keep asking the customer in satisfaction surveys whether some of the "expected needs" are met. Just define the requirements in the beginning with the customer and monitor the conformance internally. The requirement may need to be adjusted as time moves on because of changing customer needs. Save the satisfaction survey questions for those quality measures that are desirable rather than expected. See Dr. Kano's expected vs. desired vs. excited quality in Figure 3.1, page 28.

The first column in Figure 3.5 lists the basic customer needs. The second represents the weights that customers have assigned those areas. Customers do the weighting in the needs assessment. An example of a weighted importance question is:

Please distribute 100 points among the following five areas according to how important the area is to you in the purchase of this product or service:

1. _____ Order fulfillment
2. _____ Sales service
3. _____ Trade promotions
4. _____ Billing
5. _____ Product returns

100 points total

The sixth tool is best suited for customer needs assessment and satisfaction measurement among customers internal to a company.

	Need	Weight	Characteristic	Requirement
	Order fulfillment	20%	Accuracy / Timely	Return call w/i 24 hrs. / Gives access to d-base
	Sales service	30%	Responsive / Informed	90% error-free / plus/minus two days
	Trade promotions	15%	Etc. / Etc.	Etc. / Etc.
Key Customer Needs	Unloading	10%		
	Billing	20%		
	Product returns	5%		

Figure 3.5 Customer quick maps.

36 *Chapter Three*

TOOL #6: SERVICE LEVEL AGREEMENT

Each employee and department within an organization has internal customers. Customer satisfaction and conformance to requirements internally ultimately determines how well the organization delivers to external customers. The following is an example of an internal service level agreement (SLA). The process for development is much the same as it is for external customers, for instance, each internal supplier interviews the internal customer and negotiates the terms and conditions of the product/service quality, the delivery methods and times, and communication. Thus, Figure 3.6 shows a sample internal SLA table of contents.

Topic	What
1. Scope of services	• Specifically, what will the work cover?
2. Organization chart and who's who	• Who are the people and what are their relationships?
3. Flowchart	• How will the work flow?
4. Authority levels	• What approvals are required?
5. Customer requirements	• What are the regulations, laws, and specifications?
6. Processes, for instance: • Order request process • Training (customer and supplier) • Quality control and inspections • Change process	• What are the key processes?
7. Communication plan • Reports: types and frequency • Meetings: regular and special • Complaint resolution process	• How will you communicate? • How often?
8. Time and materials	• What will be the costs per unit/hour/etc?
9. Standards	• What are the standards, for instance, response time?
10. Measures	• What processes will be measured? How? When?
11. What is needed from the customer?	• What training does the customer need? What information, resources, and help will the customer provide?
12. Customer satisfaction system, e.g., measures, reviews, rewards, and recognition	• What questions will be tracked? How often?
13. Documents and records	• What are the key documents and records? • Who will maintain and control them?

Figure 3.6   Sample table of contents for internal service level agreement (SLA).

TOOL #7: DERIVED IMPORTANCE (FROM THE OVERALL SATISFACTION QUESTION)

The next section delves into customer satisfaction surveys. Every customer satisfaction survey needs to have a question that asks about "overall level of satisfaction." The reason why that question is important is because it is the most highly correlated with repeat purchase behavior in real life. If you put the question at the beginning of the survey, you will get the most honest answer—logically and emotionally. Purchase decisions do have an emotional component—even though they may be business-to-business purchases. We have all seen the most objective-looking procurement systems with written criteria and weightings that are skewed by an individual who marked the vendor or product down on all counts because of a subjective reason.

The set of overall satisfaction questions that most relates to customer loyalty is as follows (N/A stands for not applicable; use if the question doesn't apply to you or you don't know):

1. *My overall satisfaction with product or service X was:*
   ❏ *Very dissatisfied* ❏ *Dissatisfied* ❏ *So-so* ❏ *Satisfied* ❏ *Very satisfied* ❏ *N/A*

2. *I would use the service or product again.*
   ❏ *Strongly disagree* ❏ *Disagree* ❏ *So-so* ❏ *Agree* ❏ *Strongly agree* ❏ *N/A*

3. *I would recommend this service or product to others.*
   ❏ *Strongly disagree* ❏ *Disagree* ❏ *So-so* ❏ *Agree* ❏ *Strongly agree* ❏ *N/A*

On the phone you merely ask them to provide the number that most closely matches their level of satisfaction, with one = low satisfaction and five = high satisfaction. The scores can also be an average of the three loyalty questions. A respondent who gives a five on all three is 40 percent more likely to be a repeat buyer.

Customer needs can be "derived" by correlating other questions on the survey to either high or low satisfaction. The statistical technique is called *conjoint analysis*. Statistical programs like SPSS and others can correlate survey answers to ferret out the derived customer needs. You can also do it with smaller numbers of customer surveys (under 50) by using Microsoft Excel. Go to the Data Analysis selection under Tools in Excel and select "correlation." The dialog box will guide you through the steps.

BEST PRACTICE FOR CUSTOMER NEEDS ASSESSMENT

Best-practice customer needs assessment organizations take information from the "voice of the customer" wherever and whenever it occurs. The information is synthesized, analyzed, and developed into key customer requirements. Several of the following tools may be used to gather customer needs:

1. Complaint resolution system

2. Lost customer (or lost projects) measurement system

3. Quality function deployment

4. Open-ended comments from the customer satisfaction measurement

5. Moments of truth: reports on customer suggestions from sales, service, and frontline people

6. Focused interviews and/or focus groups

7. Derived importance items (determined by using conjoint analysis to see which subitems relate to overall satisfaction)

No mathematical formula or neural net analysis can assign numbers and come out with the key customer needs (yet). However, when an organization looks at all of this data simultaneously, *key needs typically leap out.* Usually customers are complaining, leaving, and commenting on similar frustrations throughout the purchase and use cycle. Thus, synthesizing these key needs and then testing them on a broader population is a best-practice method for truly understanding customers. Specifically, the organization:

1. Takes and summarizes data from as many inputs as possible—starting with systematic needs analysis

2. Synthesizes the conversational data through a verbatim analysis (some software programs can do some of this)

3. Determines the top key needs in various areas (technical, ordering, availability, delivery, communication, invoices, etc.)

4. Has a broad band of customers assign weights of importance to each need (in clusters of five)

5. Has the customers define operational requirements for success in each key category (delivery, invoice, and ordering)

6. Turns these measurable operational definitions into processes and standards within the organization

7. Measures the result of the processes against the customers' requirements

Customer Satisfaction Measures

SIX STEPS IN DEVELOPING A CUSTOMER SURVEY

Figure 4.1 details the design of a customer satisfaction survey. Please note that customers are asked what they want tracked in the needs assessment phase. In addition, questions are tested on other customers so ambiguity and confusion are spotted before the survey is given to a wide sampling.

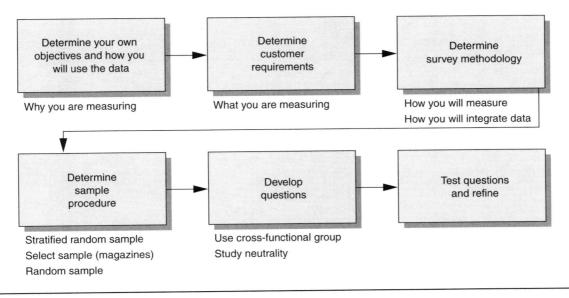

Figure 4.1 Six steps in developing a customer survey.

CUSTOMER SATISFACTION SURVEYS

As was mentioned in chapter 3, Needs Assessment, the most revealing question in customer satisfaction surveys is the question on overall satisfaction:

Please rate your overall satisfaction with product or service X.
❏ *Very Dissatisfied*   ❏ *Dissatisfied*   ❏ *So-so*   ❏ *Satisfied*   ❏ *Very Satisfied*   ❏ *N/A*

The overall satisfaction question alone is used to trend the data. You may be using "top box" or the percentage of your respondents that rate your product "very satisfied" as the main number you are tracking. You would trend the "top box" percentage every year in a trend chart. The overall satisfaction question is the most robust question in the survey because it captures the emotional and logical parts of buying. It is the question most highly correlated with repeat buying behavior. Thus, you can use this single question to benchmark various departments, locations, or even competitors. Using one common question for synthesis allows departments to customize questions and yet still compare their results.

Another "overall satisfaction" question that is helpful is one on value. For example:

Please rate the value (price vs. features) of this product/service relative to others you have tried.
❏ *Much less value*   ❏ *Less value*   ❏ *Same value*   ❏ *More value*   ❏ *Much more value*   ❏ *N/A*

The value question can be placed anywhere on the survey.

TOOL #1: POSTCARD TYPE SURVEY—EASY

This is called a postcard survey not because it is always sent by postcard (although sometimes it is), but because it usually could fit on a postcard (see Figure 4.2). The survey is simple, has from four to 10 questions, and intends to discern a basic level of customer satisfaction. This type of survey is used most often in a "scorecard" (rather than customer) focused company. It is typically done by mail, fax, or e-mail.

Granted, the postcard survey is easy and the organization does get a clue about satisfaction. But the problems with the approach in Figure 4.2 are:

1. The questions aren't actionable. (No one can replace the food that wasn't fresh—no one knows which food wasn't fresh.)

2. The questions aren't traceable. (No one knows what bill was inaccurate so no one can fix it.)

3. The questions aren't specific. (No one really knows what "friendly" means or what the scope of the unfriendly behavior was.)

4. The respondents' names aren't given. (No one knows with whom to follow up.)

5. No room is provided for comments. (This is usually the richest section for honest feedback.)

Usually customers sense that the organization doesn't really care—so these postcard-type surveys are typically thrown away. Sometimes organizations get comments back in the margins (note no section on the postcard survey shown for open comments)—most often complaints about the customer having to provide the stamp.

Joe's Food Delivery Service

Customer Satisfaction Survey

Please circle the number that best represents your level of satisfaction with our service, 1 = very low to 5 = very high.

1. Our people were friendly	1	2	3	4	5
2. The order was accurate	1	2	3	4	5
3. The food was fresh	1	2	3	4	5
4. The delivery was prompt	1	2	3	4	5
5. The bill was accurate	1	2	3	4	5

Figure 4.2 Sample of a postcard survey.

If all the organization can afford is a postcard survey; at least do three things:

1. Put a return stamp on it. Send it via e-mail or fax. Make it easy to return.

2. Put a Comment section on it.

3. Put a Name (optional) line on it with a space for a phone number so you can follow up if the customer is asking for help.

TOOL #2: WRITTEN CUSTOMER SURVEY

When customer satisfaction measurement started becoming popular in the 1980s, most organizations sent out written surveys. (See the sample written survey in Figure 4.3.) The response rates were typically 5 percent to 40 percent. Most of the time anonymity was considered important, so neither codes nor customer names allowed the researcher to nudge customers to send them back. Over time, organizations learned that it takes at least four contacts to get a decent response rate (above 70 percent). And, you might as well call because you have to call anyway to remind the customer to send the survey back. Thus, about 80 percent of experienced customer research companies have moved to phone surveys. The cost is actually less and the results are much more specific, actionable, and traceable. The initial concerns for anonymity and unbiased interviewer response proved to be more theoretical than helpful to real customer focus.

Order Selection and Delivery

(CHECK ONE)	Very Poor	Poor	Fair	Good	Very Good
1. How accurate is the selection of your order?	❏	❏	❏	❏	❏
2. How dependable is our delivery?	❏	❏	❏	❏	❏
3. How do you rate the neatness of our drivers?	❏	❏	❏	❏	❏
4. What is the condition of the products at the time of your delivery?	❏	❏	❏	❏	❏
5. What has been your experience with our in-stock performance?	❏	❏	❏	❏	❏
6. What has been your experience with our bar codes?	❏	❏	❏	❏	❏

Comments: _____

continued

Figure 4.3 Sample distribution company satisfaction survey.

Customer Service and Order Department

(CHECK ONE)	Very Poor	Poor	Fair	Good	Very Good
7. Overall, how do you rate our customer service department?	❏	❏	❏	❏	❏
8. How do you rate our crediting requests for shortages?	❏	❏	❏	❏	❏
9. How knowledgeable are our customer service people?	❏	❏	❏	❏	❏
10. Please rate how quickly your call is transferred when phoning our offices.	❏	❏	❏	❏	❏
11. How responsive are we in returning your phone calls?	❏	❏	❏	❏	❏

Comments: _____

Sales Department

(CHECK ONE)	Very Poor	Poor	Fair	Good	Very Good
12. Overall, how do you rate the usefulness of our sales representatives' visits to your store?	❏	❏	❏	❏	❏
13. How do you rate his/her merchandising knowledge?	❏	❏	❏	❏	❏
14. How do you rate his/her product knowledge?	❏	❏	❏	❏	❏

Comments: _____

Pricing

(CHECK ONE)	Very Poor	Poor	Fair	Good	Very Good
15. How do you rate our everyday wholesale prices?	❏	❏	❏	❏	❏
16. How attractive are our volume discount programs?	❏	❏	❏	❏	❏
17. How attractive are our case stack and volume purchase deals?	❏	❏	❏	❏	❏
18. Overall, how do you rate our monthly specials publication?	❏	❏	❏	❏	❏

Comments: _____

continued

Figure 4.3 Sample distribution company satisfaction survey.

Customer Satisfaction Measures **45**

Consumer Flyer Program (Looking Good, Feeling Good)

(CHECK ONE)	Very Poor	Poor	Fair	Good	Very Good
19. Overall, how do you rate the format of our flyers?	❑	❑	❑	❑	❑
20. How do you rate our product selection?	❑	❑	❑	❑	❑
21. How do you rate our retail pricing on promoted products?	❑	❑	❑	❑	❑
22. What has been your experience with our in-stock performance on flyer items?	❑	❑	❑	❑	❑
23. Overall, how do you rate the quality of our window banners?	❑	❑	❑	❑	❑

Comments: _____

Employee Courteousness and Helpfulness

How would you rate our employees regarding courteousness and helpfulness?

(CHECK ONE)	Very Poor	Poor	Fair	Good	Very Good
24. Customer service representatives	❑	❑	❑	❑	❑
25. Sales representatives	❑	❑	❑	❑	❑
26. Order desk representatives	❑	❑	❑	❑	❑
27. Telephone receptionist	❑	❑	❑	❑	❑
28. Truck drivers	❑	❑	❑	❑	❑
29. Credit department	❑	❑	❑	❑	❑
30. Buyers	❑	❑	❑	❑	❑
31. Data processing	❑	❑	❑	❑	❑
32. Management	❑	❑	❑	❑	❑

Comments: _____

Miscellaneous

(CHECK ONE)	Very Poor	Poor	Fair	Good	Very Good
33. How would you rate the range of products offered in our catalog?	❑	❑	❑	❑	❑
34. How easy to use is our catalog?	❑	❑	❑	❑	❑

Comments: _____

continued

Figure 4.3 Sample distribution company satisfaction survey.

46 *Chapter Four*

How Do We Compare?

Example:
Please write in the names of the three distributors you use most often. Evaluate each company's performance using this scale:

A = The best   D = Needs improvement

B = Above average   F = Terrible

C = Average, same as their competition   N = No opinion

Acme Distributors

Write in your primary distributor's name

Pacific Wholesalers

Write in your secondary distributor's name

Zalos Inc.

Write in the name of your third most often used distibutor

Overall customer service	F	B	C
On-time delivery	C	C	C

Write in your primary distributor's name

Write in your secondary distributor's name

Write in the name of your third most often used distibutor

35. Overall customer service			
36. On-time delivery			
37. Driver courtesy and skill			
38. Salesperson knowledge			
39. In-stock performance			
40. Order selection accuracy			
41. Resolves mistakes quickly			
42. Responsive to special needs			
43. Price			
44. Promotional programs			
45. Product selection			
46. Credit terms policies			
47. Overall impression			

continued

Figure 4.3 Sample distribution company satisfaction survey.

Customer Satisfaction Measures   **47**

continued

48. Have you taken advantage of any of our
    special services such as: (CHECK ONE)   **Yes**   **No**
    a. Price stickers   ❏   ❏
    b. Custom pricing   ❏   ❏
    c. Guidelines or reports   ❏   ❏
    d. Consumer flyer program   ❏   ❏

Comments: _____

_____   _____
Name   Phone

Figure 4.3   Sample distribution company satisfaction survey.

Tips for written surveys:

1. The less automated-looking the survey, the higher the response rate. Even though scanned surveys are much easier to process, they usually receive low response rates. Customers feel like a number so they don't consider their responses important.

2. The appropriate length of the survey varies according to how important your product or service is to the success of your customer. Many producers of customer-engineered products find that an eight-page survey gets an 80 percent response rate among their loyal customers. If the product or service is of low importance, keep it to a couple of pages.

3. Make it easy to read. Some surveys have fonts so small that older people can't read them. Others are so cluttered and unorganized that they look too complicated and time-consuming.

4. Cluster the questions in logical units. Put all the order fulfillment questions together. Put product reliability questions together. It is not only easier for your customers, but also easier for you to hand over the sections to various departments.

5. Always have a question (or two) that relates to overall satisfaction. That single question will be what you will use to trend your data over months, quarters, and/or years. (See Overall Satisfaction Questions in chapter 3, Needs Assessment.)

6. Use statistical techniques like conjoint analysis to see which questions relate best to overall satisfaction. (See Derived Importance in chapter 3, Needs Assessment.)

7. The most common scale in customer surveys is the Likert scale. A Likert scale is one that has word anchors at both ends. The sample survey in Figure 4.3 starts with a Likert scale, labeled for instance, "very poor" to "very good."

PREPARING THE CUSTOMER FOR THE SURVEY

Conditioning the customer to receive an e-mail, mail survey, phone call, or visit is a very important part of the process. No matter which media is used, it is important from the beginning of the relationship to condition the customer that their input is important. The customers are vital in designing and refining your products or services. At the conclusion of the application or contract award, you need to make your customer feedback system visible to the customer. A customer service 800 number for complaints or queries should be clearly written on all proposals, ordering documents, invoices, shipping labels, and in docking stations. Your customer measurement system needs to be part of the boilerplate of the proposal and contract. Thus, the customer is conditioned from the beginning that he or she will be part of your overall system.

About three weeks before a survey is deployed, the customer needs to be contacted by mail, phone, e-mail, or fax to reintroduce the process. The media used depends on how the survey will be done.

Phone surveys: Send an introductory letter with your letterhead on it, or e-mail in advance, to assure the customer that the survey is legitimate. If the survey is longer than 10 minutes, a secretary or researcher needs to call ahead and make an appointment.

Mail surveys: The salesperson usually contacts the customer one to two weeks ahead of the survey and lets the customer know that a survey is on its way. A personal request from the salesperson to fill it out goes a long way to increasing the response rate.

E-mail surveys: if they are short, you can include the motivation letter from the executive in the e-mail.

In-person surveys: an introductory letter should be sent first, then a secretary or researcher can call and set up the appointment.

Then make sure you keep your promises.
Sample wording to introduce the survey is shown in the following example.

Dear Customer,

We have selected you to be part of an important key customer survey because you have been a valuable customer to Company X. Every six months we select a sample of our most important customers for input into our strategic planning process. We have hired Company Y to do these phone interviews/visits so that you can be completely honest. Company Y has been doing Industry Z interviews for the past X number of years and has a good understanding of the industry. Company Y will look for patterns of issues among our important customers and tell us what is needed for improvement as well as where we are doing well.

The interview will take about 15 to 20 minutes and will be done between Month X and Month Y. The information will be reviewed by the executive committee in Month Z. We will provide a progress report on the results of the survey via an e-mail in Month Z.

Thanks for your help in serving your needs more precisely. Feel free to contact me if you have any questions or comments about the process.

Sincerely

High-Level Executive

TOOL #3: PHONE OR IN-PERSON SURVEY

Tips on Phone and In-Person Interviews

All the rules that have already been covered on being systematic and scientific apply to phone surveys. For instance, segmenting and targeting the customers, sampling, and question construction are all very similar in phone and in-person surveys. In-person interviews are usually done with just the most important customers in the Gold list because they are expensive to do. If you are working in foreign countries, though, in-person tends to be preferred by customers.

Do you *tape the interview*? Many researchers put the tape recorder on the desk in an in-person survey and say, "We routinely tape these interviews so we don't miss any details later. Feel free to turn it off if there is any part that you don't want recorded." Although there may be a moment of discomfort, that usually passes and the customer forgets about the tape. In high-tech interviews, tapes are particularly helpful because of the scientific detail. Taping a phone conversation may inhibit the respondent enough that they either don't participate or don't provide honest answers.

No-show rates on in-person interviews run very low, (usually less than ten percent), while missed interviews scheduled over the phone can run as high as 20 percent. The personality and experience of the researcher makes a significant difference in the response rate.

The main benefit to phone and in-person interviews is that you can *probe*. Both allow you to trace the source of high scores or low scores back to the specific product or service and the specific person delivering that service. In addition, the interviewer can find out exact details of either "wowing" the customer or frustrating him or her. These open-ended notes are usually the most valuable part of the measurement.

Be sure to *match the level* of the interviewer with the person being interviewed. A phone or in-person interview with a CEO needs to be done by someone who is not only able to ask questions and listen, but can probe intelligently. That means that he or she must know something about the industry. One reference that might be helpful to researchers unfamiliar with the company or industry is Hoover's Online industry profiles on the Web (www.hoovers.com).

Software

Computer aided telephone interview (CATI) software has a high payback rate in productivity. CATI software allows the researcher to mark answers on the computer as he or she interviews over the phone. Software such as SurveyPro can:

1. Cut analysis calculation time tenfold.

2. Go from the data to the report quickly.

3. Perform cross-tabs to combine information from different questions, for instance "How many owners of revision two of the product were highly satisfied versus owners of the original version?"

Web-based customer satisfaction surveys also speed analysis and synthesis. Both SurveyPro and Inquisite are Web-software programs that can be e-mailed to participants and analyzed electronically.

Verbatim Analysis: How to Analyze Qualitative Information

Phone and in-person interviews are rich in qualitative information. Qualitative information is all that information that comes from customers in their own words rather than answering multiple choice or rank-order questions. To do verbatim analysis, follow these steps:

1. Take down as much of the conversation in their words as you can.

2. Review your notes and look for categories of comments.

3. List those categories that are common to all the conversations (e.g., poor reliability, noncompetitive warranty policy, inaccessible technical help).

4. Count the number of individuals that mentioned that category.

5. Show on a graph the percent of respondents that mentioned that category (see Figure 4.4).

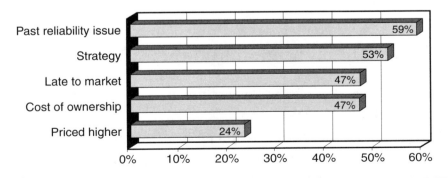

Figure 4.4 Sample interview results: key reasons for buying a competing product.

TOOL #4: E-MAIL SURVEY—EASY

E-mail surveys typically get a much higher response rate than do mail surveys (sometimes as high as 70 percent) You can ask fairly simple questions and branch (skip) to a whole subsection of a survey based on the answer given. E-mail surveys can be handy for surveying the second- and third-tier customers while giving Gold customers the more personal attention of phone or mail surveys.

Several companies now specialize in e-mail surveys, for instance:

1. Inquisite.com
2. CustomerSat.com
3. SurveyPro

Some tips on doing e-mail surveys:

1. Be sure to include a paragraph to motivate the reader to fill out the survey.
2. Design the survey so that people can go through it very quickly. Stay away from heavy graphics or fancy background templates.
3. Include a due date on the survey and introductory e-mail (usually within about 10 days).
4. E-mail surveys have a higher response rate than Web-based surveys. You lose some people who have little patience in waiting for a Web site to open.
5. Make sure you have preset intervals to analyze the data. Because analysis is almost instant, it can be tempting to show off the results before you have a critical mass of respondents.
6. Sensitive questions are best for the phone or in-person surveys, not in e-mail or Web surveys.
7. On each question allow for an answer that indicates not applicable (N/A). Also allow room for open-ended comments.

The best questions for e-mail surveys are mechanical. Multiple choice, yes/no, latest trends, feature preferences are all very suitable for an e-mail or Web survey. The least advisable questions are deeper questions that involve detail, competitor analysis, and open-ended reasons behind decisions. Telephone or in-person surveys are more suitable for finding out the rich detail that will help you develop solutions.

Complaint Resolution Systems

BEST-PRACTICE COMPLAINT SYSTEMS

Best-practice complaint systems have features that foster customer feedback. The first feature is quick access, e.g., a toll-free phone number, somebody at the site, and/or the phone number publicized on all communications. The second feature is that complaints and suggestions have a whole system designed around early resolution. That means that

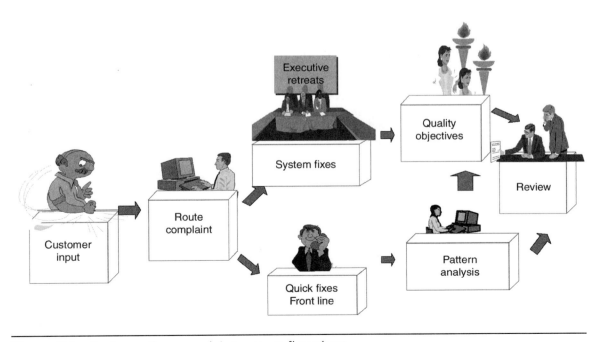

Figure 5.1 Best-practice complaint system flowchart.

process owners are already identified, and customer service employees are empowered to fix issues. Scripts also help the customer service representative resolve problems in one call.

Unless each individual and department has standards for handling customer questions and problems, a complaint resolution system call falls short for the customer. Customer relationship management software that automates resolution closure can be very helpful. Examples of software providers include Clarify, Remedy, Vantive, and Oracle (module) and others. A simple Excel worksheet or Access database can also do the same.

Table 5.1 covers some of the features to consider when selecting complaint-handling software:

Table 5.1 Complaint-handling software features.

Enabler	What It Does
ACD	Automatic call distribution. Allows waiting call to be passed to the next available service representative. Measures wait time.
AIN	Automatic identification number or caller ID. Reduces call times by 20 to 30 percent and improves interaction by identifying who is calling.
Auto screen transfer	Allows transfer of completed customer screen to other people. The customer tells the story just once.
Caseload management	Provides reminders and follow-up deadlines to improve resolution time.
FAQ	Frequently asked questions. Allows service rep to look up answers if he/she doesn't know.
Job aids	Provides diagrams, procedures, and other helpful information to the customer service rep to enable them to answer difficult questions.
Master account	Gives customer service rep ability to view customer's entire account.
Queue monitoring	Monitors wait, transfers, and abandon rates. Improves productivity by up to 60 percent. The function is automated in some phone systems.
Screen pops	Facts and questions that pop up on the screen to help the customer service rep with answers or probes.
Tracking	Tracks each problem to completion. Flags opportunities for cross-selling.
VRU	Voice response unit. Tests customer satisfaction of problem-solving process by asking a few survey questions at the end of the transaction.

CRITICAL ISSUES AND TIPS

Critical Issues	Tips
Complaint-handling software	Software such as Clarify, Vantive, Remedy, Lotus Notes, and others are worth investigating.
Collect complaints systematically	Complaints should be fixed immediately if they don't impact other customers and your budget. Immediate fixes are different from deeper, chronic issues. Pattern analysis needs to be done at systematic intervals (no more than once per quarter) by executives.
800 number and coverage	Best-in-class coverage is 24/7. Twenty-four hours a day and seven days a week is increasingly the standard for customer call centers!
Personality characteristics in hiring	Look for patience. Use position as vehicle for moving up in company.
Position of manager	The closer the CEO is to the customer service manager, the more customer focused you'll be.
Training required	Industry average is six weeks. The Marriott hotel chain and the Harris electronic company have closer to six months.
Automated answers needed	Package answers in scripts for training but customize at least part of the response in verbal or written form. Form letters are irritating to most customers. Yet, scripted answers with additional comments can be very effective.
Ownership and resolution cycle time	Corrective action needs an owner and expected fix time, and is tied to individual performance.

Analysis and Decision Making: Balanced Scorecards

ANALYSIS AND DECISIONS

The whole purpose of measuring customer satisfaction is to manage customer satisfaction. According to my own 20 years of research, customer satisfaction scores are highly related to customer loyalty and repeat buying behavior. Brad Gale reports the same results in his book, *Managing Customer Value*. Thus, customer data is used for decision support. Specifically, it is used to answer the key questions:

What are our strengths according to customer perceptions (so we can advertise areas that resonate with current customers)?

What are our weaknesses (so we can improve)?

Companies may want to benchmark their different units against the overall customer satisfaction score to see who is doing a better job. Then the highly rated units can share their processes with the lesser-rated units. Note that you may get some geographic and industry-related differences. New Yorkers tend to rate lower than southerners. High-tech and science workers tend to rate slightly lower than the rest of the world. Simply ask individuals on the phone or in person, "What would it take to get a 5 (or the highest rating)?" Another test question is, "What companies are best-in-class on this dimension? What score would you give them?" If the customer consistently responds by saying, "I won't give a 5," then you might want to raise the score to a 5 to correct for that personality trait.

58 *Chapter Six*

SAMPLE RESULTS CHART FOR CUSTOMER NEEDS

A sample results chart for customer needs is shown in Figure 6.1. Notice that the analysis is done for both needs assessment and satisfaction in percentage of respondents who wanted this feature. It could be the percentage of respondents who indicated that they were "very satisfied." Percentages are better than averages for these types of surveys because extreme scores too easily influence averages (unless the numbers in the sample are very large).

SAMPLE SATISFACTION TREND CHART

Let's take the overall satisfaction question as an illustration of how you would aggregate and analyze the results. You have 100 people complete the survey. Very dissatisfied receives a score of 1 and very satisfied a score of 5.

My overall satisfaction with the product/service was:
❑ *Very dissatisfied*   ❑ *Dissatisfied*   ❑ *So-so*   ❑ *Satisfied*   ❑ *Very satisfied*   ❑ *N/A*

This is the one question you use to either benchmark varying departments or do trend lines over the years, so it is a good place to start in analysis.

Here are the most frequently used summary measures:

	Summary Measure	Definition
1	Top box*	Percent of respondents who checked "very satisfied"
2	Top two boxes	Percent of respondents who checked "satisfied" or "very satisfied"
3	Average or mean	Add all of the scores and divide by the # of respondents
4	Bottom box*	Percent of respondents who checked "dissatisfied" or "very dissatisfied"
5	Percentage listing	The percentage who gave ratings of 1, 2, 3, 4, or 5 is displayed in a bar chart.

*Sometimes "top box" is used to mean the top two boxes. Likewise, "bottom box" can be used to mean just the lowest score. You need to check when you see these words.

Notice that the trend line is done just on the overall customer satisfaction question or an average of the three main satisfaction questions (overall satisfaction, likelihood to buy again, and likelihood to refer a friend). Also note that the best-in-class track the industry average and compare their scores to an overall standard.

Figure 6.2 is an example of a trend chart that displays the average of the customer satisfaction scores in surveys from 2001 to 2005. The straight line represents the industry average. The same type of column (or line) chart could be used to show a trend with top box or bottom box scores.

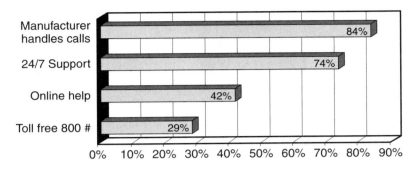

Figure 6.1 Service preferences.

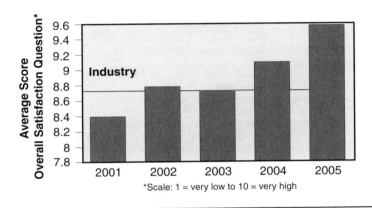

Figure 6.2 Trend chart of overall customer satisfaction results.

Notice how an average score for overall satisfaction gives you limited information. You might want to do both a top box chart and a bottom box chart. That information will help you understand the specific distribution of the satisfaction scores. You would then use a Pareto chart to detail the drivers of overall satisfaction and the drivers of dissatisfaction. If you had a bottom box score of 36 percent (that means that 36 percent of the respondents were very dissatisfied), then you need to detail why they were dissatisfied.

An example of a Pareto chart that shows some of the drivers of dissatisfaction is shown in Figure 6.3. This Pareto chart explains the drivers of overall dissatisfaction for the latest year.

Report charts that take the qualitative information from phone or in-person interviews or focus groups and translate them to quantitative measures usually use the percent of respondents who mentioned various categories (see Figure 6.4).

Detail of individual questions is usually shown in horizontal bar charts. This provides the most information about each question. Figure 6.5 shows the average of all surveys on the question, "How satisfied were you with technical support?" The average was 3.39. Note the difference in the richness of information you get in reporting the results by percentages as in 6.6. The top box in this chart would be 52 percent (percent of the respondents answering

60 Chapter Six

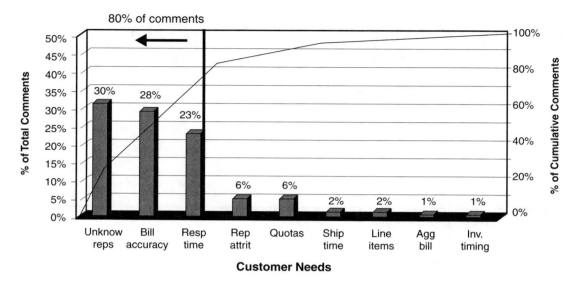

Unknow reps:	Unknowledgeable sales representatives
Bill accuracy:	Inaccurate bills
Resp time:	Responsive time; usually refers to returned phone calls
Rep attrit:	Sales representative attrition
Quotas:	Salespeople had such unreasonable quotas with such high stakes that they lied
Ship time:	Late arrival times for product
Line items:	Aggregating line items so that the invoices were unclear
Agg bill:	Customer wanted aggregate billing for all their locations; they didn't want separate bills
Invoice timing:	Customers were receiving invoices months and sometimes years after the service

Figure 6.3 Sample Pareto chart.

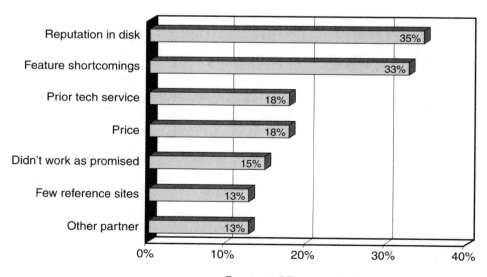

Figure 6.4 Percent of respondents that mentioned this reason for why the bid was lost.

"very satisfied"). Bottom box ("very dissatisfied) would be 36 percent. That is quite a disparity. The average chart, Figure 6.5, implies that everyone felt just OK about the technical support. Figure 6.6 shows that there are two camps, 52 percent love it and 38 percent are *very* unhappy. You would need to investigate the disparity.

The final report of interviews and written surveys needs to contain both the quantitative and qualitative results. You do that by combining the charts with comments in the customer's own words. You can do this in PowerPoint and use the Note pages. The appearance comes out better if you integrate your graph from Excel into a PowerPoint slide. Dress it up. Then paste your PowerPoint slide into a Word document and do the comment section using Word. It is helpful to take typical customer comments, find the most representative,

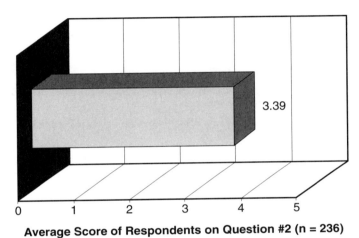

Figure 6.5 Satisfaction reported as an average.

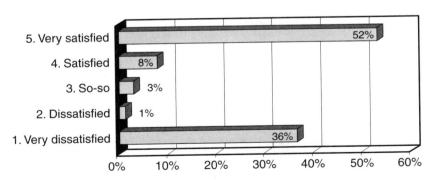

Figure 6.6 Satisfaction reported in percentages.

62 Chapter Six

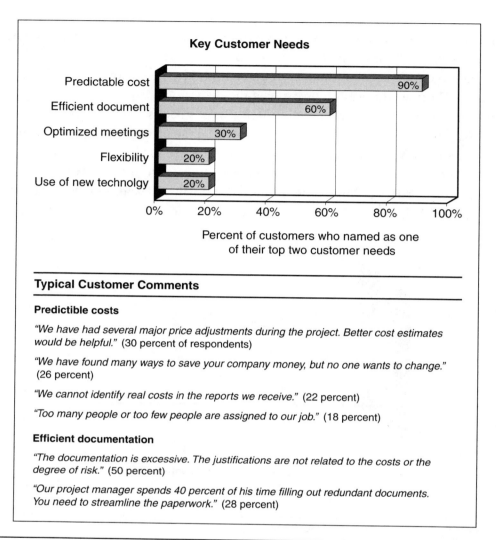

Figure 6.7 Sample needs assessment report page.

quote that directly, and then put the percentage of customers who made similar comments in parentheses after the quote. Figure 6.7 provides an illustration of a report page that can be used for both needs assessment and satisfaction surveys.

SAMPLE BALANCED SCORECARD

The balanced scorecard in Figure 6.8 illustrates how the four critical areas of results can be viewed simultaneously in the strategic quality plan retreat. Those four areas include: 1) financial, 2) customer/stakeholder satisfaction, 3) employee and supplier, and 4) operations/quality data. Only by seeing the results simultaneously can conclusions and strategy reflect the entire functioning of the organization.

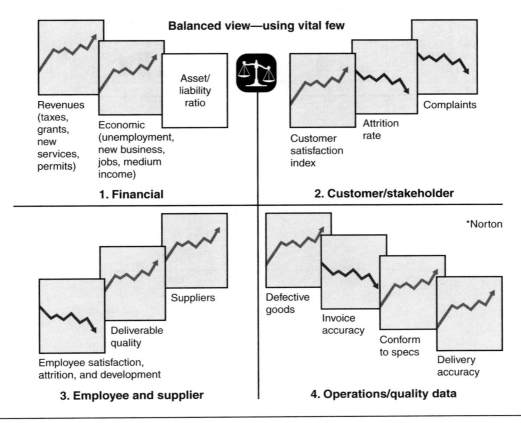

Figure 6.8 Executive retreat using a balanced scorecard.

VIEW BALANCED SCORECARD DATA SIMULTANEOUSLY

The table display shown in Figure 6.9 is a popular way of showing the data to a decision-making group and letting them see all the data simultaneously. Notice how the quantitative trend charts are coupled with Pareto charts that indicate qualitative answers. For instance, a trend chart can tell you whether you are having an increase or decrease in customer attrition. The Pareto chart will separate out the *vital few* reasons *why* customers are leaving.

64 Chapter Six

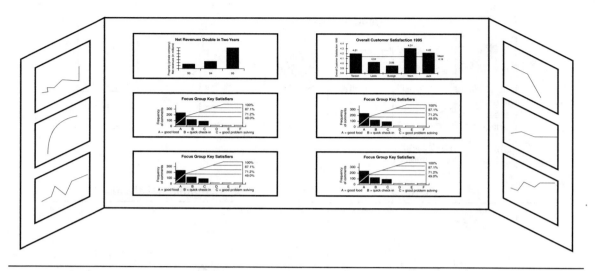

Figure 6.9 Table display of data.

Action and Review

ACTION: TURNING DATA INTO IMPROVEMENT

As indicated by ISO 9001, customer satisfaction starts with top-level executive involvement, transitions into customer needs assessment, and then cascades the understanding of these needs down through the organization. Each department and individual identifies his or her own individual responsibilities in meeting those specific needs. Executives then conclude the closed-loop process by reviewing and rewarding results. Figure 7.1 shows how top management strategy and direction cascade down the organization.

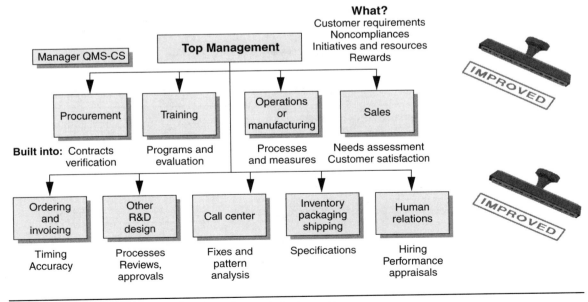

Figure 7.1 Customer satisfaction: from data to action.

The agenda in Figure 7.2 includes the requirements stipulated by ISO 9001 for management to cover in review sessions.

These review meetings are not only required, but are vital if implementation is to be taken seriously by the organization. The higher the ranks in the room, the more action will be taken from the data.

Management Review Agenda

Date: _____

Start time: _____

End time: _____

Location: _____

Facilitator: _____

Document # _____

Revision # _____

Bring: _____

_____

Attendees:	Function	To do**
1. _____	_____	____
2. _____	_____	____
3. _____	_____	____
4. _____	_____	____
5. _____	_____	____
6. _____	_____	____
7. _____	_____	____
8. _____	_____	____
9. _____	_____	____
10. _____	_____	____
11. _____	_____	____
12. _____	_____	____

Location of management
review records: _____

1. QMS Review—inputs   Person   Time   Input documents and records
   a. Follow up actions from earlier management review
   b, Status of corrective and preventive actions
   c. Results of new customer satisfaction audits
   d. Customer feedback from complaints and suggestions
   e. Performance review on customer-focused processes
   f. Changes that could affect quality management system

                                             Person   Due   Action items (include who
2. QMS Review—outputs   needs to be informed)
   a. Improvement of the product(s) related to customers
   b. Improvement of QMS: quality policy, plan, and processes
   c. Resources needed

Figure 7.2 Top management review agenda.

Appendix

This appendix provides:

1. A glossary of customer feedback tools
2. Useful vocabulary

The glossary of customer feedback tools will help you differentiate between customer satisfaction surveys, transaction surveys, perceptual surveys, and other tools. Each has a special target audience and set of benefits. One of the most frequent mistakes organizations make is selecting the wrong tool(s) for their unique objectives.

ISO 9001:2000 has very specific vocabulary the reader needs to know. Related customer satisfaction and management terms are also included.

GLOSSARY OF CUSTOMER FEEDBACK TOOLS

Surveys	Target audience	What it can do	Can't do	Population/ sample size and frequency	Best media, sampling method and expected response percent	Best scales and analysis	Examples of best types of questions
Opinion/ perception	Your customers Competitor's customers Non-users	Compare you w/other cities Gauge reputation Some needs assessment Find preferences Help segment customers Used for competitive analysis, needs assessment, and price queries	Determine nuances of customer satisfaction (have non-users in sample)	100/80 1,000/278 1 million/1000 260 million/1100 Every 3–5 yrs	Best media: phone Done blind—respondent doesn't know who sponsor is Random generation of phone numbers (within clusters) Desired response rate: 95 percent of sample	Percent of total responding in any direction by segment Conjoint analysis	Comparative questions: • *"What company comes to mind when you think of long distance phone service?"* • *"When you choose a library, what determines your decision?"*
Customer satisfaction	Heavy users of ser-vices or products— Gold customers Moderate/light users (as a separate audi-ence)—optional	Provide scorecard for overall satisfaction to use as trend line. Identify drivers of overall satisfaction. Rate individual departments as well as interdepartmental issues. Comment section: identify needs not represented in questions Rate issues that are interdepartmental (teamwork, communi-cation, etc.)	Competitor analysis New service analysis Trace problem back to specific person, shift, etc. unless done by phone or in person	Gold: everyone 2nd tier and 3rd tier: statistics charts At least once a year	Best media: phone or in-person; e-mail can supplement Best sampling method: Stratified random Desired response percent: Gold customers: 80–100% Other: 50 percent	Likert scale, e.g., (1–very dissatisfied to 5– very satisfied) Overall satisfaction question is main question tracked for trends Drivers of overall satisfaction and dissatisfaction found by doing conjoint analysis	Qualifying questions: • *"How often do you use this service?"* • *"My overall level of satisfaction with X is:"* (use Likert scale) • *Department questions are clustered together* • *Interdepartmental questions (teamwork, safety, communication, etc.) are also clustered*

continued

Surveys	Target audience	What it can do	Can't do	Population/ sample size and frequency	Best media, sampling method and expected response percent	Best scales and analysis	Examples of best types of questions
Transaction surveys	Those who have just completed a transaction, for instance: Received a bill Had a repair Registered a complaint Been to a council meeting Been to training	Ask simple satisfaction questions about a single transaction Identify good and poor service specific to individuals Identify staffing or workload issues Fix issues real time Probe about how others execute	Go into depth about policies, equipment, or desired features	Sampling of all transactions Done consistently throughout the year	In-person Voice Response Units (VRUs) By phone E-mail Sampling: random	Overall satisfaction percent top box Track people and teams who did well; # of fixes	Overall satisfaction: • *"How satisfied were you with X?"* Use Likert scale • *"What did you like?"* • *"What needed improvement?"*
Lost customers	Customers who have defected or found another alternative	Understand why they left Do competitor analysis Possibly recover some customers	Generalize results to entire customer base	Within a short time of loss (usually < 3 weeks)	Media: phone or in person Sample size: all of Gold customers; none of those you hoped would leave	Track attrition percent and recovery rates Track reasons for attrition Track recovery revenues/ profits	Reasons for defection: • *"What led to your reducing your use of X?"* • *"What/who are you using instead?"* • *"What are the reasons behind your switch?"*

continued

Surveys	Target audience	What it can do	Can't do	Population/ sample size and frequency	Best media, sampling method and expected response percent	Best scales and analysis	Examples of best types of questions
Needs assessment	Heavy users New users Lost customers Noncustomers	Get full understanding of what customers need at various points of involvement with you Be able to identify segments with various needs and provide modules of services and/or products for them Be able to prioritize needs so that key needs receive adequate resources Provide the questions that will be tracked in the customer satisfaction survey	Predict what needs will exist in the future Satisfy all needs for all parties	Every 3–5 yrs. Use weighted balance method to quantify priorities (have them give 100 points across 5 items according to their priorities)	Gather likely priorities: In-person interviews Comment section from satisfaction Lost customer reasons Complaints Moments of truth inventories Test with statistically sound sample size to see what priority needs are	Track types of needs, attributes and operational definitions Example: *Type of need:* ambulance service *Attribute:* fast *Operational definition:* arrive in 3 min	Open ended: • *"What are the critical issues that determine whether you buy Competitor A or B?"* • *"What is important to you?"* • *"What would you like us to track in a customer satisfaction survey?"* • *"If you were the CEO of this company and could change just one thing, what would it be?"* Critical incidents: Talk about a good/bad customer experience in that (bank, driving school). Probe the details.
Focus groups or focus interviews (one at a time)	Experienced users of services Brand new users of existing service or product New audience for new service or product	Learn about preferences in the nuances of the service/product Learn about installation/entry difficulties Prototype analysis; ID bugs Invent the future: brainstorm met and unmet needs	Evaluate satisfaction-group (dynamics interfere w/honesty) Generalize to entire group	Need at least 3 focus groups of 10 apiece to analyze statistically Use criteria-based selection of group members (not random)	In person as a group In person as individuals By phone (one at a time)	Verbatim analysis (distill the comments into a vital few categories and prioritize by frequency and criticality)	Invent the future: • *"What are the key challenges facing your (life, company, job)?"* • *"What services should we be offering?"* • *"How do these challenges affect this service/product?"* Test a prototype: • *"Which of choices A, B, or C do you like? Why?"*

continued

Surveys	Target audience	What it can do	Can't do	Population/ sample size and frequency	Best media, sampling method and expected response percent	Best scales and analysis	Examples of best types of questions
Moments of truth inventories	Customer comments, suggestions or com-plaints are recorded at the front line Regular synthesis follows Customer requests for unavailable products or services are logged and synthesized	Find out what customers share spontaneously as they are being serviced—good and bad Discover services that are desired but not currently offered	Be used as a scorecard	Mark on checklist as is happening Summarize and discuss monthly	In person during transaction	Track compliments and complaints, requests, confusion as they happen	Probing questions: Observation Listening to spontaneous comments and questions from customers
Advisory groups	Can be any of following: Frequent users Influential outsiders Clients	Help understand future trends Help keep pulse on the advisors' trends in their businesses Help with strategic alliances	Stipulate priorities for Gold customers	Monthly, quarterly or semiannually Usually 3 hr to 3 day meetings	People are selected to meet the objectives of the advisory group (connections, understanding of client needs, help with new product intro-duction, etc.)	Test hypotheses generated by advisory group with larger population	Preferences and trend questions: • *"What changes and challenges are going on in your industry?"* • *"Can you help us make this connection or introduce X?"*
Complaint systems	Those who have immediate com-plaints or questions Usually the more loyal the customer, the more complaints and questions he/she has Gold customers should have an escalation process. The quality of the problem-solving process is one of the key reasons why people stay or leave.	Identify possible at-risk customers Do quick fixes and identify larger, chronic patterns (policies, equip, facilities) to be fixed Make unhappy customers into loyal ambassadors Help customers understand why some requests aren't currently feasible	Resolve all complaints immediately Satisfy all needs of all customers	Cannot generalize but can include issues raised by complaints on customer satisfaction surveys—test wider population	Have someone available at easy-to-remember phone # Advertise phone # everywhere Circulate during events, training, and ask, "If you could do one thing to improve this event or service/product X, what would it be?" Use Web site for additional input	Track number and types of complaints, resolution time, contributions from employees, fixes, and chronic issue resolution Track productivity of customer service reps plus satisfaction with system	Scope questions: • *"Who?"* • *"What?"* • *"Where?"* • *"When?"* • *"How much or how bad?"* • *"What are alternatives?"* *Systems issues driving the problem (for instance training, hiring, pay, promotions, etc)*

continued

continued

Surveys	Target audience	What it can do	Can't do	Population/ sample size and frequency	Best media, sampling method and expected response percent	Best scales and analysis	Examples of best types of questions
Mystery shopping	Target population is those who are working at their job	See if standards are being met Determine consistency of service levels View obstacles for customers; for instance, poor signage, clutter, wait times, and accuracy Help management empathy for customers if lacking Ambush success Reinforce employees for meeting standards	Be main performance measurement system	Random visits are better than planned Anonymous shoppers are better than recognized	Randomly select sites to visit at random intervals.	Use checklist to evaluate various aspects of service	Checklist includes: • Signs, maps, and instructions • Help if customer confused • Clear directions • Timing of service • Friendliness of help • Accuracy of answers • User-friendly facilities • Adherence to safety rules • Adherence to standards

ISO 9000-2000 VOCABULARY

Quality Terms

capability: Ability of an organization, system, or process to realize a product that fulfills the requirements for that product.

customer dissatisfaction: Customer's opinion of the degree to which a transaction has failed to meet the customer's needs and expectations, for instance, customer complaints.

customer satisfaction: Customer's opinion of the degree to which a transaction has met the customer's needs and expectations. It is time- and event-specific and based on mutual needs and expectations and the communication between parties.

grade: Category or rank given to different quality requirements for products, processes, or systems having the same functional use—for instance, first class versus coach.

process: System of activities which uses resources to transform inputs into outputs.

product: Result of a process.

quality: Ability of a set of inherent characteristics of a product, system, or process to fulfill the requirements of customers and other interested parties.

requirement: Need or expectation that is stated, customarily implied, or obligatory.

Management Terms

management: Coordinates activities to direct and control an organization.

management system: To establish policy and objectives and to achieve those objectives. May include a quality X system, a financial X system, or customer X system.

quality assurance: Focuses on providing confidence that quality requirements are met.

quality control: Part of quality management focused on fulfilling quality requirements.

quality improvement: Focuses on increasing the effectiveness and efficiency of processes, products, and systems.

quality management: Coordinated activities to direct and control an organization with regard to quality.

quality management system: To establish a quality policy and quality objectives and to achieve those objectives. ISO may provide the basis for the establishment of policy.

quality planning: Quality management focused on setting quality objectives and specifying necessary operational processes.

quality policy: Overall intentions and direction of an organization related to quality as expressed by top management. ISO may provide the basis for this.

quality objectives: Something sought or aimed for related to quality. Should be quantitative for operations.

system: Set of interrelated or interacting elements.

top management: Person or group who directs and controls an organization at the highest level.

Organization Terms

behavioral: Courtesy, honesty, or other behaviors.

characteristics: Distinguishing features—physical, sensoral, behavioral, temporal, ergonomic, functional.

concession: Authorization to use or release a product that does not conform to specific requirements.

conformity: Fulfillment of a requirement.

corrective action: Action taken to eliminate the cause of a detected nonconformity.

correction: Action taken to eliminate a detected nonconformity. May be repair, rework, regrade.

customer organization: Unit or person that receives a product. Can be internal or external to organization, for instance, end-user, retailer, beneficiary, and purchaser.

defect: Nonfulfillment of a requirement related to an intended or specified use. Defect should be used with extreme caution because of legal implications.

dependability: Quality characteristic meaning the available performance. Reliability, maintainability, and support performance may all be part of this. Dependability is a nonquantitative term.

design and development: Set of processes that transforms requirements into specified characteristics and into other specifications of the product realization process. Design and development can be two stages.

deviation permit: Authorization to depart from the originally specified requirements of a product prior to realization, for a limited quantity of product or period of time for a specific use.

ergonomic: Psychological characteristic, e.g., easy-to-use, safe, related to human being.

functional: How well the device functions. Example: distance range of an airplane.

infrastructure: System of permanent facilities and equipment of an organization.

interested party: Person(s) having an interest in the success of the organization. Can be a bank, society, or other institution.

nonconformity: Nonfulfillment of a requirement.

organization: A group of people and facilities with an orderly arrangement of responsibilities, authorities, and relationships.

physical characteristics: Characteristics that pertain to the human body, matter, or energy. This includes chemical, electrical, biological, or mechanical characteristics. An example is the human body is 70 percent water.

preventive action: Action taken to eliminate the cause of a potential nonconformity or other potentially undesirable situation.

procedure: Specified way to carry out an activity or process. May or may not be written or documented.

process: System of activities which uses resources to transform inputs to outputs. Usually carried out under controlled conditions to add value.

product: Result of a process. Hardware, software, services, and processed materials are the four kinds of products. It may depend on the dominant element as to what it is called.

project: Unique process consisting of a set of coordinated and controlled activities with a start and finish date. Projects are undertaken to achieve an objective conforming to specific client requirements, including timetables, cost, and resource allocations. Client requirements may evolve as the project progresses.

quality characteristics: Inherent characteristic of a product, process, or system derived from a requirement.

sensory characteristics: Related to smell, touch, taste, sight, hearing. The taste of the orange is sweet.

service: Intangible product that is the result of at least one activity performed at the interface between the supplier and the customer, for instance, repair of a car, delivery of knowledge.

software: Intellectual product consisting of information on a support medium. Software can be in the form of concepts, transactions, or procedures. A computer program is software.

special process: A process where the conformity of the product cannot be readily or economically verified.

supplier: Person(s) that supply a product. Can be internal or external to customer's organization.

temporal: Pertaining to or limited by time.

traceability: Ability to trace the history, application, or location of that which is being considered. The traceability of hardware may relate to the origin of materials and parts, the processing history (which processing plant beef came from). Traceability may also mean ability to trace the completion of the project.

work environment: Set of conditions under which a person operates.

Customer Satisfaction Terms

bottom box: The percent of respondents that answered the lowest category (e.g., very dissatisfied). Sometimes bottom box includes the bottom two categories (e.g., very dissatisfied or dissatisfied).

customer quick map: Map that traces customer needs through attributes and operational definitions.

discovery interviews: Needs assessment interviews to discover what conscious and unconscious customer needs are.

inquisite: Web-enabled customer satisfaction survey software.

Likert scale: A scale used on surveys that usually has five, seven, or 10 points and is anchored at both ends by words such as "very dissatisfied" and "very satisfied."

operational definition: A definition of a customer need that permits you to measure success operationally.

ServQual: A survey method that measures both importance and satisfaction.

SPSS: Survey software that enables question development and statistical analysis.

stratified random sample: A sampling process that entails stratifying your population into groups or clusters, and then randomly sampling within each cluster.

top box: Usually means either the top score or top two scores on a question. For a scale of 1–5 (1 = very dissatisfied to 5 = very satisfied), the top box would mean the percent of respondents who answered 5. Sometimes top box is used to mean percent that answered 4 or 5.

weighted distribution: A scale that allows the respondent to distribute 100 points across (usually) five attributes according to how important that attribute is. That score is the importance weight.

Bibliography

The following books are some of the best books on customer satisfaction measurement.

Allen, Derek R., and Morris Wilburn. *Linking Customer and Employee Satisfaction to the Bottom Line*. Milwaukee: ASQ Quality Press, 2002.

Allen, Derek R., and Tanniru R. Rao. *Analysis of Customer Satisfaction Data: A Comprehensive Guide to Multivariate Statistical Analysis in Customer Satisfaction, Loyalty, and Service Quality Research*. Milwaukee: ASQ Quality Press, 2000.

Fowler, Floyd J., Jr. *Improving Survey Questions: Design and Evaluation*. Thousand Oaks, CA: Sage Publications, 1995.

Johnson, Michael D., and Anders Gustafsson. *Improving Customer Satisfaction, Loyalty, and Profit: An Integrated Measurement and Management System*. San Francisco: Jossey-Bass, 2000.

Kessler, Sheila. *Measuring and Managing Customer Satisfaction: Going for the Gold*. Milwaukee: ASQC Quality Press, 1996.

Lavrakas, Paul J. *Telephone Survey Methods: Sampling, Selection, and Supervision*. Thousand Oaks, CA: Sage Publications, 1993.

Mentzler, John T., Carol C. Bienstock, and Kenneth B. Kahn. "Benchmarking Satisfaction: Market Leaders Use Sophisticated Processes to Measure and Manage Their Customers' Perceptions," *Marketing Management* 4, no. 1 (summer 1995): 41–46.

Myers, James H. *Measuring Customer Satisfaction: Hot Buttons and Other Measurement Issues*. Chicago: American Marketing Association, 2001.

Naumann, Earl, and Kathleen Giel. *Customer Satisfaction Measurement and Management: Using the Voice of the Customer*. Cincinnati, OH: Thomson Executive Press, 1994.

Schuman, Howard, and Stanley Presser. *Questions and Answers in Attitude Surveys*: Experiments on Question Form, Wording, and Context. Thousand Oaks, CA: Sage Publications, 1996.

Stewart, David. "Focus Groups: Theory and Practice." In *Applied Social Research Methods Series*, Vol. 20; Thousand Oaks, CA: Sage Publications, 1990.

Sudman, Seymour, and Norman M. Bradburn. *Asking Questions*. San Francisco: Jossey-Bass, 1982.

Vavra, Terry. *Customer Satisfaction Measurement Simplified: A Step-by-Step Guide for ISO 9001:2000 Certification*. Milwaukee: ASQ Quality Press, 2001.

TRAINING—SEMINARS AND WEB TRAINING

Brandt, Randy. *Measuring and Managing Customer Satisfaction*. American Society for Quality. 800-248-1946. Three-day seminar.

Kessler, Sheila. *Customer Satisfaction: ISO 9001:2000 Compliance*. American Society for Quality. 800-248-1946. Two-day seminar.

Kessler, Sheila. *Measuring and Managing Customer Satisfaction: ISO 9001:2000 Compliance* (Web course). Quality Web-Based Training. 850-916-9436 or www.qualitywbt.com.

Index

Note: Italicized page numbers indicate illustrations.

A
advisory groups, 71

B
balanced scorecard, 62–64
Baldrige Award, 2
    criteria, 1
    study, *2*
bar charts, horizontal, 59, 61
best-in-class tools, 3–4
best practice
    complaint systems, 53
    customer needs assessment, 38
    flowchart, 53
branching questions, 21

C
clustering, 22
comment cards, 4, 6
complaint resolution, 6, 53–55
    critical issues and tips, 55
complaint systems, 71
complaint-handling software features, *54*
computer aided telephone interview (CATI), 51
confidence level, 13, 15
conjoint analysis, 37, 47
customer needs assessment, 5, 27–38
    report page, sample, *62*
    results chart, sample, 58–59
    satisfaction trend chart, sample, 58–59
customer quality, types of, 27–28
customer quick map, 35
customer relationship managing software, 54
customer satisfaction, 28, 65
    flowchart, *12*
    index, 21
    managing, 57
    measuring, 57
    plan, 11–12
    responsibility matrix, 12

surveys, 4–5, 39, 67, 68
    system, *11*
    top management review agenda, *66*
    trend chart, *22*
customer specifications, 29
    sample, *29*
customers, measuring, 7–13
    scientific approach, 13
    systems approach, 8–12

D
derived importance, 37, 47
desired quality, 27–28
discovery interviews, 33–34

E
easy tools, 3–4
    problems, 4
easy vs. best-in-class
    complaint resolution systems, 6
    customer needs assessment, 5
    customer satisfaction surveys, 5
e-mail survey, 48, 52
error of the mean, 13
excited quality, 27–28
expected quality, 27–28

F
focus groups, 70

H
Harris polls, 15
Hoover's Online industry profiles, 50

I
in-person survey, 48, 50
Inquisite, 51
ISO 9001:2000 standard
    customer-related changes, 2
    key components, 2

79

major changes, 3
ISO audit, 11
ISO standards
difference between ISO 9000, ISO 9001, and ISO 9004, 3

K

Kano, Dr. Noriaki, 27

L

Likert scale, 21, 24, 47
lost customers, 69

M

mail survey, 48
management responsibility, 1
management review, 65–66
management review agenda, *66*
moments of truth inventories, 71
multiple choice scale, 24
mystery shopping, 72

N

needs assessment
discovery interviews, 33–34
report page, sample, 62
survey, 70

O

open-ended questions, 23
opinion/perception survey, 68
overall customer satisfaction questions, 21–22
overall satisfaction, 40, 47

P

paired-choice scale, 25
Pareto chart, 59
sample, *60*
perceptual surveys, 67
phone survey, 48, 50
postcard survey, 41–42

Q

qualifying questions, 20–21
qualitative analysis, 51
qualitative information, how to analyze, 51
quality function deployment, 30, 32
quality management principles, 3
question construction, 19–23
confidentiality and expectations, 19
content of questions, 19–20
qualitative measures, 19–20
sensitive information, 19
sequence of questions, 19
types of questions, 20–23
question design, errors made in, 23

R

random sampling, 14
stratified, 14
rank order scale, 25
report charts, 59
sample, *60*
request for comments, 23
response rates, 17–18
increasing, 18
responsibility matrix, 12

S

sample size, 15
sample specifications, *29*
sampling methods, 14
scale construction, 24–26
scorecards, 9
segmenting your customers, 7–8
service level agreement, 36
ServQual, 30
needs assessment sample, *31*
skip box questions, 21
software, 52, 54, 55, 61
statistical sampling, 13–15
statistics, 13
stratified random sampling, 14
survey
construction, 16
example, *49*
introducing, 48
media, 48
survey organization and logic checklist, *16*
SurveyPro, 51
systematic measures, 8–10
systems approach to measuring customers, 8–10

T

toolkit guidelines, 1–2
transaction surveys, 67, 69
trend chart, 22, 58, *59*

V

value question, 40
verbatim analysis, 51
voice of the customer, 38
voice response units, 5

W

Web survey, 21
weighted distribution scale, 26
weighted importance, 25–26
question, 35
written customer surveys, 43–37
tips, 47
written surveys, 21, 23, 29–31, 43–47

Y

yes/no question, 25